GETTING STARTED
WITH FRENCH

GETTING STARTED WITH FRENCH

Beginning French for Homeschoolers and Self-Taught Students of Any Age

WILLIAM E. LINNEY

BRANDON SIMPSON

ARMFIELD ACADEMIC PRESS

Published by Armfield Academic Press

Editorial consultants: Annie Bourque, Edouard Hesse,
Leigh C. Simpson

Editorial assistants: Sidonie Wade, Geraldine Linney

ISBN: 978-1-62611-005-2

CONTENTS

PREFACE

My first book, *Getting Started with Latin*, was a labor of love. I wrote it to help homeschooled and self-taught students learn beginning Latin at home, without a teacher. Since the publication of *Getting Started with Latin*, the response has been positive (except for that one nasty email I got a few years back). People seem to like the one-thing-at-a-time format of the book, which never leaves them lost and wondering what just happened like other books do. This is significant because homeschooled and self-taught students are a special group of people who need specialized materials—products that allow them to learn at home without access to a teacher who specializes in that particular subject. So, when I saw the positive response to *Getting Started with Latin*, I wondered if I could also apply that same step-by-step approach to a modern language such as Spanish. While I was writing *Getting Started with Latin*, my old friend Antonio Orta and I joked around about writing a Spanish book together when I was finished with the Latin book, and that's how we ended up writing *Getting Started with Spanish*. Then I got to know Brandon Simpson, and we decided to write *Getting Started with French* together.

This book is designed to accomplish several educational goals. We have designed this book to:

- Be self-explanatory, self-paced, self-contained and inexpensive
- Allow the student to make progress with or without a French teacher
- Provide plenty of practice exercises after each new concept so that the student can master each idea before moving on to the next one
- Provide audio recordings for aural practice and supplementary instruction
- Avoid making beginning French any more difficult than it actually is

Getting Started with French was created to meet the unique needs of home-schooled and self-taught students. It is self-contained, with no extra materials to purchase (such as pronunciation tapes, answer keys or teachers' editions). It's also in a large format to make it easier to use, and non-consumable so it can be used with multiple children. The answer key is in the back of the book, and there are free pronunciation recordings and authors' commentary recordings available for download at www.GettingStartedWithFrench.com. In this book, new words and concepts are introduced in a gradual yet systematic fashion. Each lesson provides many exercises for practicing the new material while reviewing material from previous lessons.

Getting Started with French makes beginning French accessible to students of any age or educational background. Because this book moves so gradually, students probably will not say *This is too hard for me. I quit!* Instead, these bite-size lessons leave the student encouraged and ready to continue. But when you do finish this book, don't let your French studies end there. Learning and using a foreign language is quite a thrill—so keep going, and above all, have fun with it!

William E. Linney

HOW TO USE THIS BOOK

This book is structured around one main teaching method: Teach one concept at a time and let the student master that concept before introducing the next one. With that in mind, read the tips listed below to help you use this book to the greatest advantage.

THE NEW WORD

Start each lesson by observing the new word for that particular lesson. All French words in this book are in **bold print** so they will be easy to recognize. The meaning of the new word is in *italics*. In some lessons you will learn a new concept and in others you will simply review material from previous lessons.

PRONUNCIATION

The best way to learn correct pronunciation is by listening and copying what you hear. Visit www.GettingStartedWithFrench.com to download the free pronunciation recordings in MP3 format. In these recordings, each new word and exercise is read aloud by a native speaker from Paris, France. You may listen to these recordings on your computer or other listening device. These free audio recordings will help you achieve proper French pronunciation.

Sometimes, French words sound absolutely nothing like the way they look. For this reason, some lessons will have a written description of how to pronounce that lesson's new word (that's the part of the lesson called Pronunciation Tip). The purpose of these tips is not to tell you exactly how that word sounds—instead, it's to give you a general idea of how the word sounds and to help you avoid common pronunciation errors. Also, there is a pronunciation chart on page 278 for the sake of reference.

GRAMMATICAL INFORMATION

If needed, a lesson may contain an explanation of how to use the new word introduced in that lesson. Charts and examples are used to give the reader a clear presentation of the French grammar knowledge needed for that particular lesson.

Our website, www.GettingStartedWithFrench.com, has special audio commentary recordings which have been prepared by the authors. These recordings cover each lesson in detail, so if you have any trouble understanding the material presented in a lesson, you will have plenty of help on hand.

THE EXERCISES

Armed with the knowledge of the new word and how to use it, begin to translate the exercises. In a homeschool environment, it is probably best to have students write their answers in a notebook. Older students and adults may prefer to do the exercises mentally. Next, turn to the answer key in the back of the book to see if your translations are correct. By comparing the French and the English, you will learn from your mistakes. Translating the exercises over and over will enhance learning and speed your progress.

PRACTICING CONVERSATIONAL SKILLS

Now comes the really important part. Once you understand the exercises, it's time to practice using what you have learned. The ideal situation would be to have a family member or friend with whom you can practice French on a daily basis. Repetition is the key here. Try repeating the exercises over and over to each other or making up your own similar sentences. We have tried to make the vocabulary in this book pertain to common everyday activities such as being, going, eating, etc., so that you can take what you learn here and immediately begin to use it in actual conversations.

If you can't practice with a friend or family member, you can still accomplish a lot by practicing with the pronunciation recordings. You can practice your pronunciation skills by trying to pronounce the exercises just like the speaker. Or, you can practice your listening skills by repeatedly listening to and interpreting the recordings.

FRENCH COMPOSITION

For an additional challenge, you can try to translate the answers back into French using the knowledge you have gained from that lesson. This is called French composition. Figuring out how to write something in French can be a great learning tool because it requires you to think about the material in a different way. Try it and see! Again, it is probably best to write these exercises in a notebook.

DON'T PUT THE CART BEFORE THE HORSE

Do not skip ahead to a future lesson. Because each lesson builds directly on the preceding lessons, do the lessons in the order given. If you start to feel lost or confused, back up a few lessons and review. Or, take a break and come back to the material at a later time. Remember that review and repetition are essential when learning any language. One of the best things you can do to improve your understanding of French is to review the lessons repeatedly.

STAY FLEXIBLE

Everyone has a different learning style, so use this book in ways that fit your needs or the needs of your students. You can learn French as a family, on your own, or in a homeschool environment. Be creative! You could even have one night of the week when the entire family is only allowed to speak French. Who knows? You may think of a way to use this book that no one else has thought of (putting it under the short leg of the kitchen table does not count).

TESTS AND QUIZZES

To give a student a test or quiz, simply back up to a previous lesson. Have the student translate those exercises without looking at the answers. Then, the teacher or parent can grade the exercises using the answers in the back of the book. Another possibility would be to test the student's listening skills by having him or her translate the exercises directly from the audio recording for that lesson.

SCHEDULING

Some homeschool parents like a lot of structure in their teaching schedules, while others prefer a less structured learning environment. Depending on your personal preferences, you may either plan to cover a certain number of lessons in a certain period of time, or allow your students to determine their own pace. It's up to you.

HOW MUCH TIME PER DAY?

A few minutes a day with this book is better than longer, less frequent sessions. Thirty minutes a day is ideal for language study. Of course, this may vary with each student's age, ability, and interest level.

SELF-TAUGHT ADULTS

Adults who use this book will enjoy the freedom of learning French whenever and wherever they please. High school and college students may use it to get a head start before taking a French class, to satisfy curiosity, or to try something new. Busy adults may use it to study at lunchtime, break time, or while commuting to work (as long as someone else is driving the vehicle). The short lessons in this book will fit any schedule.

SURF THE NET!

The website that accompanies this book (www.GettingStartedWithFrench.com) has free resources to aid you in your study of French. Be sure to check it out!

LESSON ONE

PRONUNCIATION

When it comes to learning French, the first thing we need to discuss is pronunciation. No matter what language you study, learning to make the right sounds with your mouth is an important part of the learning process. But with the French language, getting the pronunciation right is even more crucial because French has an unusual pronunciation that sets it apart from the other languages in its language family. There are certain sounds in the French language that English speakers never use—so when learning French, an English speaker must learn to make these sounds for the first time. If you don't make these authentic French sounds, the words you say won't really sound French. Therefore, if you are going to be a successful student of French, you need to accept a simple fact: you are going to have to make sounds which you find unfamiliar and unusual.

In this book we are going to give you everything you need to achieve correct pronunciation. But we need you, the reader, to do some things to contribute to the learning process. Here's how you can help:

1. Be ready and willing to open up your mouth and practice making new, unfamiliar sounds. Don't be afraid to experiment!

2. Practice being a good listener. Learn to listen to the pronunciation recordings carefully, in a detail-oriented manner. Try to hear exactly how the words sound so that you can try to copy those sounds. You must first have an accurate idea of how a word sounds before you can copy it.

3. Listen to yourself carefully, too. Learn which sounds happen when you move your tongue and lips into different shapes and positions. Analyze those sounds to see if they match the sounds you are hearing.

These skills will take you a long way toward developing an authentic French pronunciation.

Be sure to visit www.GettingStartedWithFrench.com to download the free pronunciation recordings in MP3 format. In these free audio recordings, each new word and exercise is read aloud by a native speaker. You may listen to these recordings on your computer, or on an MP3 player. If you wish, you may put them on a CD and listen to them on any CD player.

LESSON TWO

WORDS DON'T SOUND THE WAY THEY LOOK

French words usually don't sound the way they are spelled (from the perspective of an English speaker). For example, when a consonant comes at the end of a word, that consonant is often silent.

Let's see how this works by examining a couple of French words.

pas

The word **pas** is pronounced something like *pah*. As an English speaker, you might look at the word **pas** and expect it to sound like the English word *pass*. But in the word **pas**, the *s* at the end of the word is silent, and the word ends with an *ah* sound.

Here's another example:

béret

The word **béret** sounds something like *beh-ray*. The *t* at the end of the word is silent. And, the word ends with an *ay* sound, not a *t* sound as you might expect.

Take some time to practice pronouncing **pas** and **béret**. Listen carefully to the pronunciation recordings. Try to become accustomed to not pronouncing the consonant at the end of each of these words.

LESSON THREE

ARTICLES

Articles are words such as *the*, *a*, and *an*. Let's take a look at some examples:

The man
The woman
A chair
An apple

A noun is a person, place, or thing. In each of the examples above, we used an article to introduce each noun.

In the next few lessons, we will learn how to use articles in French.

LESSON FOUR

GENDER

In French, each noun is either masculine or feminine. This quality that nouns have is called *gender*.

This concept is easy to understand with people and animals—after all, we know that animals and people are either male or female. But in French, even words for non-living things have gender. For instance, pencils, cars, and houses all have gender in the French language.

So whenever you learn a French noun, you must memorize the gender of that particular word—that is, whether it is masculine or feminine.

LESSON FIVE

NEW WORD   **un**

MEANING   *a / an*

PRONUNCIATION TIP: The *n* in **un** is silent—well, not exactly silent. You don't pronounce it as you would pronounce an *n* in an English word. Instead, the *n* here gives the vowel sound in **un** a nasal-sounding quality. Therefore, the word **un** sounds something like *eh* or *uh*.

In the last lesson, we learned that French nouns are either masculine or feminine in gender. In French, articles (words like *the, a,* or *an*) are also either masculine or feminine. So, if you have a masculine noun, and you want to introduce it with *a* or *an*, you must use a masculine article. Likewise, if you want to introduce a feminine noun, you must use a feminine article.

Un, our new word for this lesson, is the masculine form of the word *a/an*. Soon we will use **un** to introduce a masculine French noun.

LESSON SIX

THE R SOUND

English speakers make an *r* sound by moving the tongue to the upper rear part of the mouth and vibrating the vocal cords. Take a moment to experiment with this sound. Think about the movements you make inside your mouth as you pronounce an *r* sound.

In French, however, the *r* sound is made in a completely different manner—by lifting the back of the tongue and pushing some air through, so that it makes a noise like a gurgling or gargling sound (the tip of your tongue is anchored behind your bottom teeth). So, whenever you see a French word with an *r* in it, you must get accustomed to making that gurgling *r* sound at that point in the word instead of the *r* sound you have been making your whole life! And remember, this kind of *r* sound is not the rolled *r* that you would find in Spanish—that's a completely different thing altogether.

Take a few minutes now to listen to the recordings that accompany this lesson so you can experiment with making this important sound.

Once you can make the French *r* sound, the next step is to try to incorporate it into the pronunciation of actual words. This will take some practice. As you pronounce French words, imagine lifting the back of your tongue whenever you need to make an *r* sound, instead of lifting your tongue toward the top of your mouth as you would when pronouncing an English *r* sound. It's a completely different movement, and to get accustomed to it you must replace the old sound and tongue movement with the new sound and tongue movement, building a new pronunciation habit.

Let's start out by practicing the following words slowly, taking them syllable by syllable. At first, practice each syllable separately, then practice saying the sequence of sounds faster and faster until you can blend them together smoothly into one word.

First let's try a word that begins with an *r*.

Renée *(ruh-nay)*

To pronounce the word **Renée**, start out with the gurgling *r* sound (lightly). Then, an *uh* sound, and then finish the word with a *nay* sound.

Here's a word with an *r* in the middle—the capital of France.

> **Paris** *(pah-ree)*

To pronounce the word **Paris**, start out with a *pah* sound, then make the gurgling *r* sound (lightly), then finish with an *ee* sound.

Finally, here's a word with an *r* at the end.

> **noir** *(nwar)*

To pronounce the word **noir**, start out with an *n* sound. Then make a *wah* sound. Finish with the gurgling *r* sound (lightly).

Keep in mind that the French *r* sound is a gentle, subtle sound—so be gentle with it, and try not to make it sound too rough or harsh. Again, listen carefully to the recordings and try to copy what you hear.

EXPRESSIONS FRANÇAISES

Have you ever visited a new place and suddenly had the strange feeling that you had been there before? If so, you have experienced **déjà vu**.

The word **déjà** means *already*. **Vu** means *seen*. So, **déjà vu** literally means *already seen*.

LESSON SEVEN

NEW WORD **garçon**

MEANING *boy*

PRONUNCIATION TIP: Notice that the letter *c* in **garçon** has a little tail hanging down from it. That tail is called a *cédille* in French or a *cedilla* in Spanish. In French, when the letter *c* comes before the vowel *o*, the *c* would ordinarily have a hard *c* sound (like the *c* in *cat*). But the *cédille* overrides this rule and makes the *c* have a hissing *s* sound. Therefore the word **garçon** sounds something like *gahr-soh*.

Garçon is our first French noun. It is masculine, so if you want to put the article *a* in front of it, you must use the masculine form, which is **un**.

EXERCISES:

1. **Garçon**
2. **Un garçon**

When you see the exercises in each lesson, try to translate them on your own. The answers are in the back of the book to keep you from peeking. And don't forget to listen to the pronunciation recordings, too.

The answers to this lesson are on page 232.

LESSON EIGHT

NEW WORD   **une**

MEANING   *a / an*

PRONUNCIATION TIP: The *n* in **une** is not silent, so go ahead and pronounce it. Keep your lips rounded as you pronounce this word. The *u* sounds somewhat similar to the *ew* in the word *few*.

You already know that **un** is the masculine form of *a/an*. Now it is time to learn the feminine form.

Une, our new word for this lesson, is the feminine form of the article *a/an*. In the next lesson, we will use **une** to introduce a feminine French noun.

In the meantime, please take a moment to examine this simple chart.

MASCULINE	**un**
FEMININE	**une**

Remember: the *u* in **un** and the *u* in **une** do not sound alike. Make sure you don't pronounce them the same.

LESSON NINE

NEW WORD   **fille**

MEANING   *girl*

PRONUNCIATION TIP: The *ll* in **fille** sounds somewhat like the *y* in *yes*, so **fille** sounds something like *fee-yuh*.

Fille is our first feminine French noun. Since it is feminine, if you want to put *a* or *an* in front of it, you must use the feminine form which is **une**.

EXERCISES:

1. **Fille**
2. **Une fille**
3. **Garçon**
4. **Un garçon**

Answers on page 232.

10

L E S S O N   T E N

NEW WORD   **et**

MEANING   *and*

PRONUNCIATION TIP: The letter *t* in **et** is silent, so **et** sounds something like *ay.*

EXERCISES:

1. **Fille et garçon**
2. **Garçon et fille**
3. **Une fille et un garçon**
4. **Un garçon et une fille**
5. **Une fille**
6. **Un garçon**

Answers on page 232.

LESSON ELEVEN

NEW WORD   **le**

MEANING   *the*

PRONUNCIATION TIP: The word **le** sounds something like the beginning of the English word *look* but with your lips in a rounded shape.

In lesson 3 we learned that articles are words such as *the*, *a*, and *an*. Articles introduce nouns. We already know how to say *a* and *an* in French, and now it's time to learn how to say *the*.

Le, our new word for this lesson, is the masculine form of the word that means *the*. We use it to say *the* before masculine nouns.

EXERCISES:

1. **Le garçon**
2. **Un garçon**
3. **Une fille**
4. **Une fille et un garçon**
5. **Un garçon et une fille**
6. **Le garçon et une fille**
7. **Une fille et le garçon**

Answers on page 232.

LESSON TWELVE

NEW WORD   **frère**

MEANING   *brother*

PRONUNCIATION TIP: The word **frère** sounds something like the word *prayer*, but you replace the *p* sound with an *f* sound.

Frère is masculine, so it needs to have a masculine article such as **un** or **le**.

EXERCISES:

1. **Frère**
2. **Le frère**
3. **Un frère**
4. **Le garçon et une fille**
5. **Une fille**
6. **Une fille et un garçon**
7. **Un garçon**
8. **Une fille et le garçon**

Answers on page 233.

LESSON 13

NEW WORD   **la**

MEANING   *the*

La is the feminine version of **le**. We use it to say *the* before feminine nouns.

Examine the following chart:

MASCULINE	**le**
FEMININE	**la**

Now you know how to say *the* before both masculine and feminine nouns. Let's get some practice with all the articles you know by translating the following exercises.

EXERCISES:

1. **La fille**
2. **La fille et le garçon**
3. **Le garçon et la fille**
4. **Le garçon**
5. **Une fille et un garçon**
6. **Un garçon et une fille**
7. **Le frère**
8. **Un garçon**
9. **Une fille**
10. **Un frère**

Answers on page 233.

LESSON 14

THE "CAREFUL" RULE

A few lessons ago we learned that when a French word ends with a consonant, that consonant is often silent. But there are some exceptions to this rule.

If a word ends with any of the consonants *c, r, f,* or *l,* the final consonant is usually pronounced. Here's a little trick to help you remember these four letters. If you put *c, r, f,* and *l* together, they (sort of) spell the word *careful* (you have to put in the vowels yourself).

Here are some examples of words that end with *c, r, f,* or *l.*

>**lac** (pronounced something like *lahk*) LAKE
>**soir** (pronounced something like *swahr,* with a very light, gurgling *r* sound at the end) EVENING
>**soif** (pronounced something like *swahf*) THIRST
>**il** (pronounced something like *eel*) HE

There are a few exceptions to the "careful" rule, but don't worry about those right now—we will tell you about them when we run into them.

LESSON 15

NEW WORD   **sœur**

MEANING   *sister*

PRONUNCIATION TIP: The word **sœur** sounds something like *seh* but with an *r* sound at the end.

Sœur is a feminine noun, so it needs to have a feminine article such as **une** or **la**.

Notice that in the word **sœur**, the letters *o* and *e* are joined, forming one character. When two letters are joined in this manner, it's called a *ligature*.

EXERCISES:

1. **La sœur**
2. **Une sœur**
3. **Une sœur et un frère**
4. **Une fille**
5. **Le garçon**
6. **Un frère et une sœur**
7. **La sœur et le frère**
8. **La fille**
9. **Le frère et la sœur**
10. **Une fille et un garçon**

Answers on page 233.

LESSON 16

SMOOTH PRONUNCIATION

The human mouth likes to say words in a smooth, coordinated fashion. For this reason, we sometimes make small adjustments to the spelling and pronunciation of words to make them easier to pronounce clearly. An example of this would be the English words *a* and *an*. They are actually two variations of the same word—the difference is that *a* comes before words that begin with a consonant sound and *an* comes before words that begin with a vowel sound. Here's an example of how this works:

> <u>A</u> nut
> <u>An</u> acorn

This variation in spelling is done in order to make the words easier to say, and it also makes them sound clearer to whomever is listening. For example, it is easier to say and understand *a nut* than *an nut*. Likewise, it is easier to say and understand *an acorn* than *a acorn*. This is because it is easier for your mouth to pronounce sounds clearly and distinctly *when the sounds alternate between consonant sounds and vowel sounds.*

Try to experience this for yourself by saying the following word combination:

> A acorn

When you say *a acorn*, you must pronounce two identical vowel sounds in a row, which is rather awkward to pronounce clearly. The solution to this problem is to introduce the word *acorn* with the article *an*, like this:

> An acorn

This creates a vowel/consonant/vowel pattern which is much easier to pronounce. Try this word combination, too:

> An nut

17

When you say *an nut*, you have two *n* sounds in a row, which is difficult to pronounce clearly. The solution to this problem is to introduce the word *nut* with the article *a*.

A nut

Take a few moments to practice the examples given in this lesson until you are sure you understand this important concept. It's important because the French language uses similar changes in spelling to make pronunciation easier—and over the next few lessons we are going to spend a lot of time studying the specifics of how these spelling changes are done.

EXPRESSIONS FRANÇAISES

Every year in New Orleans, Louisiana, there is a big party called **Mardi Gras**. But have you ever wondered what **Mardi Gras** means?

Mardi means *Tuesday*, and **gras** means *fat*. So, **Mardi Gras** literally means *Fat Tuesday*. In Christian tradition, the forty days leading up to Easter are a period of prayer, fasting, and giving to the poor. This period of time, known as Lent, starts on Ash Wednesday. Therefore, your last chance to eat whatever you want before the fasting starts is on a Tuesday—Fat Tuesday!

Large sections of North America were settled by French explorers. These explorers gave French names to many places such as Illinois, Detroit, Des Moines, Baton Rouge, and New Orleans. In Louisiana, French was spoken throughout much of the state. The use of French declined in Louisiana during the 20th century, but it is now viewed as a unique cultural trait that should be preserved and celebrated.

LESSON 17

PRACTICING SMOOTH PRONUNCIATION

To get you thinking about how alternating between vowel sounds and consonant sounds makes pronunciation easier, let's try a little experiment. In each of the exercises below, try to figure out whether you should use *a* or *an*.

As you do, don't just sound it out to figure it out, also think about the sequence of vowels and consonants and how this sequence affects pronunciation. What sequence of vowels and consonants results from choosing the correct answer? Likewise, what would happen if you chose the incorrect answer?

EXERCISES:

1. A / an elephant
2. A / an big dog
3. A / an quarter
4. A / an hour from now
5. A / an new coat

Answers on page 234.

LESSON 18

MEANING   *friend*

Let's learn a new word in this lesson—well, actually two new words: **ami** and **amie**. Even though these words are spelled differently, they are pronounced the same.

Both of these words mean *friend*, but you would use **ami** if the friend is male and **amie** if the friend is female. Since **ami** is a masculine noun, you must introduce it with a masculine article such as **le** or **un**. And since **amie** is a feminine noun, you must introduce it with a feminine article such as **la** or **une**.

Until now, all the nouns you have learned start with consonants. So, when you introduce them with **le** or **la**, it results in a consonant/vowel/consonant pattern, like this:

le garçon

Ami and **amie**, our new words for this lesson, are special because they are the first nouns you have learned that begin with a vowel. What would happen if we introduced one of our new words for this lesson, **ami**, with the article **le**? You would get this:

le ami

That would give you two vowel sounds in a row—the vowel sound at the end of **le**, and the vowel sound that begins the word **ami**. And, as we have learned in the past few lessons, when you have two vowel sounds in a row, it's harder to say and understand. This means that **le ami** gives us a problem—a problem that we will learn to fix in the next lesson.

LESSON 19

ELISION

In the last lesson we learned the words **ami** and **amie**. Also we learned that if we introduce these words with **le** or **la**, it's awkward because you must pronounce two vowel sounds in a row, like this:

le ami

In French, we use a technique called *elision* to fix the awkwardness of having two vowel sounds next to each other. Elision is when you leave out one or more letters.

Here is how we will apply elision to **le ami**:

1. Take away the *e* at the end of the word **le**
2. Replace the *e* with an apostrophe
3. Push the two words together into one word (this is called *contraction*)

Here's what you get:

l'ami

Now that **le** and **ami** have been combined into one word, you should pronounce them together as one word, like this: *lah-mee*.

The same thing would happen for **la** and **amie**, like this:

l'amie

Elision occurs all the time in French, so watch out for it as we go along. We will see it with many word combinations in the future.

LESSON 20

PRACTICING WITH ELISION

In the last lesson, you learned that elision is when you leave out one or more letters. In French, when you have a vowel sound at the end of one word and also at the beginning of the next word, elision is usually used to leave out one of the vowel sounds.

Now that you know what elision is, let's get some practice working with it. In the exercises below we have given you some new French nouns. For each exercise, do the following steps:

1. Remove the vowel from the end of **le** or **la**.

2. Replace that vowel with an apostrophe.

3. Push the words together into one word.

Work out the exercises on a separate sheet of paper, then check the answer key to see how you did.

EXERCISES:

1. **le enfant** *(the child)* L'enfant
2. **la orange** *(the orange)* L'orange
3. **le arbre** *(the tree)* L'arbre   "uh"
4. **le ordinateur** *(the computer)* L'ordinateur
5. **la image** *(the image)* L'image

Answers on page 234.

LESSON 21

ENCHAÎNEMENT

French pronunciation is smooth, connected, and continuous. One element of French pronunciation that makes this possible is called **enchaînement**. Let's use the following example to observe how enchaînement works.

une amie

When you pronounce these words, you might be inclined to leave a space between **une** and **amie** to indicate that they are two separate words. But that's not the way French is pronounced. The correct way is to pronounce the *n* sound in **une** as though it were the beginning sound of the word **amie**. This makes the words run together, eliminating any space between words. Here is what it might sound like:

ew-namie

In this way, enchaînement helps the French language to maintain a smooth, continuous pronunciation.

LESSON 22

LIAISON

By now, you are accustomed to the fact that many French words have a silent consonant at the end of the word, and you have practiced not pronouncing these silent consonants. But, under certain circumstances, these normally silent consonants can become active and are fully pronounced. This phenomenon, called **liaison**, is the subject of this lesson.

Liaison can happen when both of the following circumstances are true:

1. When a word ends with a silent consonant (or nearly silent consonant)
2. The next word begins with a vowel sound

Under these circumstances, the normally silent consonant at the end of the first word becomes active and is no longer silent. This consonant is now pronounced as the beginning sound of the next word. In this manner, liaison creates a smooth, connected pronunciation, making the sounds alternate between vowel sounds and consonant sounds.

Now that you know what liaison is, let's see how liaison works with some actual French words. We learned that in the word **un**, the *n* is not fully pronounced, but instead just gives the vowel sound of **un** a nasal quality. Therefore, if you use **un** to introduce a word that starts with a consonant, such as **garçon**, you would have a vowel/consonant/vowel pattern, like this:

un garçon

This is fine just like it is, and nothing needs to change. But what if you use **un** to introduce a noun that starts with a vowel sound, such as **ami**? That would give you this:

un ami

In this situation there would be two vowel sounds in a row—the word **un**, which is pronounced as a vowel sound, and then the sound of the *a* at the beginning of the word **ami**. And that's awkward.

That's where liaison comes in. Liaison helps to solve this awkwardness by changing the letter *n* at the end of the word **un** from a (sort of) silent, nasalizing letter to a fully pronounced *n* sound—and when we pronounce it, we pronounce it as the first sound of the next word.

Let's apply liaison to **un ami** and see what happens.

un ami (uh-namee)

Now that we are pronouncing **un ami** as *uh-namee*, there is a nice, smooth alternation between vowel sounds and consonant sounds.

In the exercises below, figure out whether the *n* at the end of the word **un** would be pronounced fully or whether it is (sort of) silent, nasalizing the vowel. Also, give the reason why.

EXERCISES:

1. **un garçon**
2. **un arbre**
3. **un frère**
4. **un ami**
5. **un enfant**

Answers on page 234.

LESSON 23

MORE ABOUT LIAISON

In the last lesson, we learned that liaison is when you pronounce a consonant at the end of a word which is normally either silent or nearly silent. Liaison helps to smooth out French pronunciation. But according to the rules of French, there are certain places where you are not permitted to have a liaison between two words, even if it looks like it would be a good idea. These places are called *forbidden liaisons*. Here's an example of what we mean:

et une

Here, you might think to yourself something like this: The *t* in **et** is silent, and the next word, **une**, starts with a vowel—therefore there will be a liaison, and I must pronounce the *t* at the end of **et**, which would sound something like:

eh–tewn

This seems like a good idea—but according to the rules of French, you can't make a liaison with the word **et**. This is a forbidden liaison. No matter what happens, the *t* in **et** will be silent.

LESSON 24

NEW WORDS   **mon / ma**

MEANING   *my*

In French, the word for *my* has both a masculine form and a feminine form. **Mon** is the masculine form, so use it with masculine nouns like **frère**. **Ma** is the feminine form of the word **mon**. Use **ma** with feminine nouns such as **fille** and **sœur**.

Mon is similar to the article **un** because the *n* at the end of the word **mon** is not fully pronounced. Instead, it gives the *o* in **mon** a nasal sound, so **mon** will sound something like *moh*.

And remember what we told you about liaison—whenever the word **mon** comes before a word that starts with a vowel, go ahead and pronounce the *n* at the end of **mon** as though it begins the next word, like this:

> **mon ami** (moh-namee)

Get some practice working with **mon** and **ma** in these exercises.

EXERCISES:

1. **Mon frère**
2. **Mon ami**
3. **Ma sœur**
4. **Mon frère et ma sœur**
5. **Un ami et ma sœur**
6. **La fille et le garçon**
7. **L'ami**
8. **Un ami**
9. **Une amie**
10. **Une amie et un ami**

Answers on page 234.

LESSON 25

MORE ABOUT MON

In the last lesson, we learned about the words **mon** and **ma**. **Mon** is masculine and **ma** is feminine. In the exercises, we used the feminine word *ma* with **sœur**, which begins with a consonant. But what would happen if you used the word **ma** with a word that begins with a vowel?

ma amie

That gives you two vowel sounds in a row, which is a no-no. Therefore, in this situation, the masculine form **mon** is used, even though **amie** is feminine.

mon amie

It may seem strange at first to use the masculine **mon** with the feminine noun **amie**, but you'll get used to it with practice. And remember that it's for a good reason—to make French pronunciation sound smooth and connected.

EXERCISES:

1. **Mon ami**
2. **Mon amie**
3. **Ma sœur**
4. **Ma sœur et mon ami**
5. **Le garçon et la fille**
6. **Une fille et ma sœur**
7. **Mon frère et mon amie**
8. **L'ami et l'amie**
9. **Un ami et mon frère**
10. **Mon amie et ma sœur**

Answers on page 235.

LESSON 26

NEW WORDS   **fils / fille**

MEANING   *son / daughter*

PRONUNCIATION TIP: The *s* at the end of the word **fils** has a hissing *s* sound. **Fils** sounds somewhat like the English word *feast*, but without the *t* sound at the end.

You already know that the word **fille** means *girl*, but **fille** can also mean *daughter*. So, if you see the word **fille**, how do you know whether it means *girl* or *daughter*? The answer is to look at the context—that is, the way the word is being used in the sentence. Let's say, for example, you see this:

> The **fille** went to the store.

It is perfectly normal to say *the girl went to the store*, but a lot less likely that someone would say *the daughter went to the store*. Therefore, if you saw a sentence like this one, you could judge from the context that the word **fille** here probably means *girl*, not *daughter*. Here's another example:

> My **fille** went to the store.

Here, the use of the word *my* changes the context, or the way the word is being used. It is perfectly normal to say *my daughter went to the store*, but less likely that someone would say *my girl went to the store*. Therefore, if you saw a sentence like this one, you could judge from the context that the word **fille** here probably means *daughter*, not *girl*.

To summarize, if you see **fille** being introduced by une or la, it probably means *girl*, and if you see it being introduced by a possessive word like *my, your, his, her,* etc., it probably means *daughter*.

GIRL

DAUGHTER

EXERCISES:

1. **Mon fils** MY SON
2. **Ma fille** MY DAUGHTER
3. **Une fille** A GIRL
4. **Ma fille et mon fils** MY DAUGHTER AND MY SON
5. **Mon fils et un garçon** MY SON AND A BROTER
6. **Ma sœur et ma fille** MY SISTER AND MY DAUGHTER
7. **Mon amie et ma sœur** MY FRIEND AND MY SISTER
8. **L'ami et le garçon** THE FRIEND AND THE BROTER
9. **Mon frère et mon ami**
10. **Ma sœur et une fille**

Answers on page 235.

30

LESSON 27

NEW WORDS   **ton / ta**

MEANING   *your*

A few lessons ago, we learned that the French word for *my* has both a masculine form and a feminine form. **Mon** is masculine and **ma** is feminine.

The French word for *your* is the same way—it has both a masculine form and a feminine form. **Ton** is the masculine form, so use it with masculine nouns like **frère**. **Ta** is the feminine form, so use it with feminine nouns like **fille** and **sœur**.

Ton is similar to **un** and **mon** because the *n* at the end of the word **ton** is not fully pronounced. Instead, this letter *n* gives the *o* in **ton** a nasal sound, so **ton** will sound something like *toh*.

And remember what we told you about liaison—whenever the word **ton** comes before a noun that starts with a vowel, pronounce the *n* at the end of **ton** as though it begins the next word. This will give you a smooth, connected pronunciation.

With **mon** and **ma**, we saw that if the next word starts with a vowel, whether masculine or feminine, you must use the masculine form **mon**. The same thing happens with **ton** and **ta**. Observe the following example:

>   **ton amie**

Amie is feminine, but since it starts with a vowel, you must use the masculine **ton** before it.

EXERCISES:

1. **Ton ami**
2. **Ta sœur**
3. **Ton amie**
4. **Ton frère et ta sœur**
5. **Ta fille et ma fille**

31

6. **Un ami et une amie**
7. **Ta fille et mon fils**
8. **Le garçon et mon amie**
9. **L'amie**
10. **Une fille et un garçon**

Answers on page 235.

EXPRESSIONS FRANÇAISES

You've probably heard the expression **bon appétit** often enough to know that it means, more or less, *enjoy your meal*. The word **bon** means *good* and **appétit** means (as you might guess) *appetite*. So, **bon appétit** literally means *good appetite*. By the way, the *t* at the end of **appétit** is silent.

When sharing a drink, English speakers might clink their glasses together and say *cheers!* In French, you would say **santé**, which really means *health*.

L E S S O N 2 8

SINGULAR AND PLURAL

Singular means there is one of something.

Plural means there is more than one of something.

Just for practice, try to figure out if the underlined word in each sentence is singular or plural.

EXERCISES:

1. I have three <u>cats</u>.
2. Hand me that <u>book</u>, please.
3. I saw a <u>deer</u> in the woods.
4. I want to catch a <u>fish</u>.
5. There are many <u>cars</u> on the road today.
6. I need a new <u>pair</u> of pants.
7. The <u>deer</u> are eating all of my plants!
8. We don't have any more <u>cookies</u>.
9. The <u>fish</u> are in the fishbowl.
10. We painted the wrong <u>house</u>.

Answers on page 236.

LESSON 29

PLURAL NOUNS

In the last lesson, we learned the difference between singular and plural. In French, so far, we have studied only singular nouns. But in this lesson, we are going to study plural nouns.

To make a noun plural, we simply add an *s*. Here's an example:

ami *(friend)* becomes **amis** *(friends)*

If a word already ends with an *s*, we don't add another one. Here's an example:

fils *(son)*

Since **fils** already ends with an *s*, to make it plural we will *not* add another *s*—instead we will just leave it as it is. Therefore, the singular form is **fils**, and the plural form is also **fils**. You will know if **fils** is singular or plural by the context in which it is used.

There are some French nouns that have different rules for making them plural. But these nouns are less common, so we will learn about them as we go along.

For now, practice making each of the words in the exercises below plural.

EXERCISES:

1. **garçon**
2. **ami**
3. **sœur**
4. **amie**
5. **frère**
6. **fille**
7. **fils**

Answers on page 236.

LESSON 30

GROUPS OF MIXED GENDER

The French word for a male friend is **ami**. The word for a female friend is **amie**. A group of only male friends is a group of **amis**. And a group of only female friends is a group of **amies**. But what happens if you have a group of friends that includes both males and females? What word would you use for them?

If a group of friends includes both males and females, you would use the word **amis**, the masculine plural form, to refer to them. This is true even if the group of friends is mostly female, with only one or two males. This is just how the rules of French grammar work (the same rule exists in Spanish, too).

LESSON 31

PLURAL ARTICLES

We have already studied how to say *the* in French. The masculine singular form is **le**, and the feminine singular form is **la**. So, there is a different word for masculine *the* and feminine *the*.

But in the plural, there isn't a masculine *the* and feminine *the*. Instead, it's the same word for both genders, and that word is **les** (it sounds something like *lay*). Observe the word **les** being used to introduce both masculine and feminine plural nouns:

> **les garçons** *(the boys)*
> **les filles** *(the girls)*

This handy chart shows both the singular and plural forms of *the*.

	SINGULAR	PLURAL
MASCULINE	**le**	**les**
FEMININE	**la**	**les**

Knowing the word **les** will give you a chance to get more practice working with liaison. Usually the *s* in **les** is silent, like this:

> **les filles** (pronounced *lay fee* with a very soft *y* sound at the end)

But if the next word starts with a vowel, there will be a liaison between **les** and the next word. You will pronounce the *s* in **les** with a *z* sound, as though it is the first sound of the next word, like this:

> **les amis** (pronounced *lay-zahmee*)

The key to mastering liaison is practice, so stick with it and you will improve over time.

EXERCISES:

1. **Les garçons**
2. **Les amis**
3. **Les fils**
4. **Les sœurs**
5. **Ton ami**
6. **Ton amie et mon frère**
7. **Ma fille et ta sœur**
8. **Le garçon et la fille**
9. **Une amie**
10. **L'amie**

Answers on page 236.

LESSON 32

NEW WORD **homme**

MEANING *man*

PRONUNCIATION TIP: The *h* in **homme** is silent. Therefore the word **homme** sounds something like *umm*.

Homme, as you might expect, is a masculine noun. **Homme** begins with an *h*, but since the *h* is silent, we will treat the word **homme** as if it starts with a vowel.

If the article **un** comes before it, there will be a liaison between **un** and **homme**, and you will pronounce the *n* in **un** as though it were the first sound of the next word. That would give you this:

> **un homme** *(eh-numm)*

If the article **le** comes before it, there will be elision between **le** and **homme**. That would give you this:

> **l'homme** *(lumm)*

And if the plural form, **hommes**, is introduced by the article **les**, there will be a liaison between **les** and **hommes**, giving you this:

> **les hommes** *(lay-zumm)*

And don't forget, the *s* at the end of **hommes** is silent.

EXERCISES:

1. **Un homme**   "uh numm"
2. **L'homme**
3. **Les hommes**   "lay-zumm"
4. **Mon fils et ma sœur**

38

5. **Ton frère et ma fille**
6. **Les amies**
7. **Les amis**
8. **Mon amie**
9. **L'amie**
10. **Les garçons et les filles**

Answers on page 237.

LESSON 33

NEW WORD **femme**

MEANING *woman / wife*

PRONUNCIATION TIP: **Femme** sounds something like *fahm*. It does not rhyme with *slim*.

A few lessons ago we learned that the word **fille** can mean either *girl* or *daughter*, and that you must use the context (the way the word is used) to determine which meaning it has.

Femme, our new word for this lesson, is the same way. It can mean either *woman* or *wife*, depending on the way it is used. If you see it introduced by an article like *the* or *a*, it probably means *woman*. If you see it with a possessive word like *my*, *your*, or *his*, it probably means *wife*.

And since you know how to say *wife*, you should also know how to say *husband*. That's the masculine noun **mari**.

EXERCISES:

1. **La femme**
2. **Ma femme**
3. **Ma femme et l'homme**
4. **Les femmes et les hommes**
5. **Mon mari et ma fille**
6. **L'homme et mon ami**
7. **Ton fils et ma fille**
8. **Les sœurs et un frère**
9. **Les amies**
10. **Une fille**

Answers on page 237.

LESSON 34

NEW WORDS   **mes / tes**

MEANING   *my* (plural) / *your* (plural)

PRONUNCIATION TIP: The *s* at the end of each of these words is silent. But if the next word starts with a vowel sound, due to liaison you will pronounce the *s* at the end of each of these like a *z*.

We have already studied how to say *my* in French. There is the masculine form **mon**, and the feminine form **ma**. So, there is a different form for masculine *my* and feminine *my*.

But when it is plural (that is, more than one thing is being possessed), it's the same word for both masculine *my* and feminine *my*. And that word is **mes**. Observe the word **mes** being used to introduce both masculine and feminine plural nouns:

> **mes frères** *(my brothers)*
> **mes sœurs** *(my sisters)*

And it's the same situation with the word *your*. There is the masculine form **ton**, and the feminine form **ta**. So you have a different form for masculine *your* and feminine *your*.

But when it is plural (that is, more than one thing is being possessed), it's the same word for both masculine *your* and feminine *your*. And that word is **tes**. Observe the word **tes** being used to introduce both masculine and feminine plural nouns:

> **tes frères** *(your brothers)*
> **tes sœurs** *(your sisters)*

Before we move on to the exercises, a quick reminder about pronunciation: the *s* at the end of **mes** and **tes** is silent—but if the next word starts with a vowel, there will be a liaison between **mes** or **tes** and the next word. In cases like these, you will pronounce the *s* in **mes** or **tes** with a *z* sound, like this:

41

mes amis (pronounced *may-zamee*)
tes amis (pronounced *tay-zamee*)

Get some practice working with **mes** and **tes** in the following exercises.

EXERCISES:

1. **Mes fils**
2. **Tes filles**
3. **Tes amis**
4. **Tes sœurs et mes frères**
5. **Mon mari et tes amis**
6. **L'homme et ta sœur**
7. **Ta femme et ma fille**
8. **L'ami**
9. **Les frères et les amies**
10. **Une fille et un garçon**

Answers on page 237.

LESSON 35

NEW WORD   **parent**

MEANING   *parent*

PRONUNCIATION TIP: **Parent** looks the same as the English word *parent*, but it doesn't sound the same. Instead, it sounds something like *par-ah*. Also, the singular form and plural form sound the same.

The word **parent** can be masculine or feminine, depending on whether it's referring to a mother or a father. In this book, we will just use it in the plural, as the word **parents**. When it's plural, it's always masculine in gender.

EXERCISES:

1. **Les parents**
2. **Mes parents et tes parents**
3. **Tes filles et un garçon**
4. **Ton fils et ton mari**
5. **Les femmes et l'homme**
6. **Les amis**
7. **Ma femme**
8. **Ta sœur et tes amies**
9. **Mes filles et ton frère**
10. **L'ami**

Answers on page 238.

LESSON 36

NEW WORD   **enfant**

MEANING   *child*

PRONUNCIATION TIP: The final *t* in **enfant** is silent, so it sounds something like *ah-fah*, with nasal vowel sounds.

Enfant can be either a masculine noun or a feminine noun. **Un enfant** means *a (male) child*, and **une enfant** means *a (female) child*. The spelling of **enfant** does not change.

In English, the words *child* and *children* can be used in two ways. One way refers to young people, as in people who are not yet adults.

This movie is for <u>children</u>, not grown-ups.

But the words *child* and *children* can also mean *offspring*, as in sons and daughters.

My wife and I have three <u>children</u>: two daughters and a son.

And the French word **enfant** is the same way—it can mean either *young people* or *offspring*. You will know which one it means by considering the context—that is, the way it is being used in the sentence.

EXERCISES:

1. **Les enfants** THe
2. **Mes enfants** my
3. **Ma fille et tes amies** M
4. **Mes parents et mon mari** My
5. **Tes sœurs et les enfants** Your
6. **Mon fils et les garçons** M
7. **L'enfant et la femme**
8. **Ta femme et tes sœurs** Your
9. **Un homme et une femme** A
10. **Ma femme et mon frère** My

Answers on page 238.

44

LESSON 37

NEW WORD   **des**

MEANING   *some*

PRONUNCIATION TIP: The *s* in **des** is silent, so it sounds something like *day*.

A while ago, we learned that the articles **le** and **la** were singular, and that they both share the plural form **les**.

Well, guess what? **Un** and **une** can be plural, too. The plural form of both **un** and **une** is **des**.

The singular articles **un** and **une** mean *a* or *an*. But their plural form, **des**, translates into English as *some*. In the following examples, let's compare the use of **un** and **des**:

> **un garçon** *(a boy)*
> **des garçons** *(some boys)*

Now let's compare **une** and **des**:

> **une fille** *(a girl)*
> **des filles** *(some girls)*

Here's a handy chart to help you remember these different forms:

	SINGULAR	PLURAL
MASCULINE	**un**	**des**
FEMININE	**une**	**des**

A reminder about liaison: If the word after **des** starts with a vowel, the *s* in **des** will not be silent—you will pronounce it with a *z* sound, as though it is the first sound of the next word.

EXERCISES:

1. **Un homme**
2. **Des hommes**
3. **Une femme**
4. **Des femmes**
5. **Mon frère et ma sœur**
6. **L'homme et la femme**
7. **Les sœurs et les frères**
8. **Tes amis et des filles**
9. **L'amie et ma fille**
10. **Mon mari, mes fils et des garçons**

Answers on page 238.

LESSON 38

MORE ABOUT ARTICLES

At the very beginning of this book, we learned a little something about articles. We learned that <u>articles</u> are words like *the*, *a*, and *an*, and we learned to use them to <u>introduce nouns</u>. Now, as we move ahead to the next steps of French grammar, we need to tell you some additional information about articles. In this lesson we want to discuss the difference between definite articles and indefinite articles.

In English, the word *the* is called the *definite article*. Why? Because when you use it, you are referring to a definite thing. Here's an example:

> Please go into the garage and get <u>the</u> broom.   *(DEFINITE)*

When you make a statement like this, it is clear that you are referring not to just any broom—instead, you have a specific broom in mind, and you want someone to go and get it! You are referring to a definite thing, therefore *the* is a definite article. In French, **le** and **la** are <u>definite articles.</u>

Even when plural, the definite article still works the same way.

> Please go into the garage and get <u>the</u> brooms.

Here, even though you are referring to more than one broom, you still have specific brooms in mind. In French, the plural <u>definite article</u> is **les**.

In English, the words *a* and *an* are called *indefinite articles*. Why? Because they don't refer to any specific item. Instead, they just refer to any item that fits the description. Here's an example:

> Please go into the garage and get <u>a</u> broom.

When you make a statement like this, you are not referring to any specific broom. In fact, there may be several brooms in the garage, and you are just asking someone to go and pick one—any broom will do. The thing you are asking for is indefinite, therefore *a* and *an* are <u>indefinite articles</u>. In French, **un** and **une** are indefinite articles.

47

The word *the* can be used to talk about something singular or something plural. In other words, the word *the* functions as both a singular article and a plural article. But *a* and *an* cannot function as plural articles the way the word *the* can. You cannot say *a brooms* or *an apples*. So, if you are an English speaker, what do you do when you need a plural indefinite article? When we need an indefinite article to be plural, we express the plural-ness of it by using the word *some*. Here's an example:

Please go into the garage and get <u>some</u> brooms.

When you make a statement like this, you are not using the word *some* as the opposite of the word *all*, as if to say, "Don't get all of the brooms—make sure you leave a few behind." That's not the point. Instead, the word *some* here is functioning as a plural indefinite article—in other words, a plural form of *a* or *an*. What you mean is that it doesn't matter which brooms the person gets—he or she just needs to get several or a few brooms. In French, the plural indefinite article is **des**.

If we were to put this all in a chart, here is what it would look like:

	SINGULAR	PLURAL
DEFINITE ARTICLE	the (**le, la**)	the (**les**)
INDEFINITE ARTICLE	a, an (**un, une**)	some (**des**)

Take a few minutes to think this over, and in the next few lessons we will give you some practice working with **des**.

LESSON 39

NEW WORDS   **bonjour / au revoir**

MEANING   *good day / goodbye*

Bon means *good* and **jour** means *day*, so **bonjour** literally means *good day*. For an English speaker, greeting someone by saying *good day* might sound a little old-fashioned, but that's how we will translate **bonjour** in the answer key just so you can remember that it's a daytime greeting.

When you answer the phone, you don't say **bonjour**. You say **allô**, which simply means *hello*.

In the expression **au revoir**, the word **au** translates as *until*. The verb **voir** means *to see* or *seeing*. Add the prefix **re-** to the beginning of **voir**, and you get the verb **revoir** which means *seeing again*. Therefore, **au revoir** literally means *until seeing again*. But we translate it into English as *goodbye*.

Other common greetings are **bonsoir** which means *good evening* and **bonne nuit** which means *good night*.

Other common French sayings that include the word **bon** are **bon voyage** which means *have a good trip* and **bonne chance** which means *good luck*.

EXERCISES:

1. **Bonjour, mon ami.**
2. **Au revoir, mon fils.**
3. **Mes sœurs et des filles.** my sisters + some girls
4. **Des amis et mon frère.** some friends + my brother
5. **L'ami.** the friend
6. **Bonne nuit, mon frère.** goodnight my brother
7. **L'homme et la femme.** the man + the woman
8. **Ta sœur et les filles.** your sister + the girls/daughters
9. **Bonsoir, mon frère.** good evening my brother
10. **Tes filles.** your daughters

Answers on page 239.

LESSON 40

NEW WORDS   **père / mère**

MEANING   *father / mother*

In addition to **père** and **mère**, you should also know the less formal words for *father* and *mother*. **Papa** means *dad* and **maman** means *mom*. The *n* at the end of **maman** is (sort of) silent, giving the vowel a nasalized sound.

EXERCISES:

1. **Mon père.**
2. **Ta mère.**
3. **Ton père et ta mère.**
4. **Bonjour, papa.**
5. **Au revoir, maman.**
6. **Les hommes et les garçons.**
7. **Mes sœurs et ta fille.**
8. **Une amie et ma mère.**
9. **L'homme et tes frères.**
10. **Des garçons et mes fils.**

Answers on page 239.

LESSON 41

SUBJECTS AND VERBS

In any sentence, the two most important elements are the subject and the verb. Let's take a moment now to think about subjects and verbs.

A noun is a person, place, or thing. The subject of a sentence is the noun that is doing the action in the sentence. In each of the following examples, the underlined word is the subject of the sentence.

> <u>Matthew</u> kicked the ball.
> <u>Canada</u> is a large country.
> <u>Flowers</u> need sunshine.

Now let's talk about verbs. Verbs are words that tell us what the subject of the sentence is doing. Verbs can be action words such as *dance, shout, walk, talk,* or *write*. Or, they can be verbs of being or existing such as *is, are, was, were,* and *will be*. Verbs of being are also called *linking verbs*. Let's look at those same sentences again, this time underlining the verb in each sentence.

> Matthew <u>kicked</u> the ball.
> Canada <u>is</u> a large country.
> Flowers <u>need</u> sunshine.

For practice, see if you can identify the subject and the verb of each of the following sentences.

EXERCISES:
1. Kate walks to school every day.
2. My car is red.
3. My sister likes ice cream.
4. The horse is brown.
5. Harry told me a joke.
6. On Thursdays, Bob plays softball.
7. Mark plays the trumpet.

8. My brother never cleans his room.
9. Julia loves bedtime stories.
10. The students finished their homework.

Answers on page 239.

EXPRESSIONS FRANÇAISES

In the movies or on TV you may have heard someone say *I now bid you **adieu**.*

Adieu is a combination of two words. The first word is **à**, which means *to*. **Dieu** means *God*. So, **adieu** literally means *to God*, but it translates into English as *good-bye* or *farewell*.

Of course, **au revoir** also means *goodbye*. But **adieu** and **au revoir** have different meanings. **Au revoir** means something like *until I see you again*, so it is used for non-permanent goodbyes (like saying *see you later* in English). **Adieu**, on the other hand, is actually a shortened version of the archaic French saying *I commend you to God*. Therefore, **adieu** is what you say when you will never see someone again. How sad!

LESSON 42

PRONOUNS

A pronoun is a word that can take the place of a noun. Pronouns are words like *he, she, it, I, we, you,* and *they.* We often use pronouns when we have already used a certain noun once and do not want to say that same noun again. Observe this example:

> Susanne is wearing a blue dress. <u>Susanne</u> bought it last week.

Instead of repeating the word Susanne in the second sentence, we can replace it with a pronoun, like this:

> Susanne is wearing a blue dress. <u>She</u> bought it last week.

In this way, pronouns can help us avoid repeating the names of the things or people we are talking about.

In each of the following exercises, try to identify the pronoun. And, if the pronoun is taking the place of another word, identify that word also.

EXERCISES:

1. Alfred's room is a mess because he never cleans it up.
2. Jeff does not like going to the locker room because it is too smelly.
3. She already took out the trash.
4. The kids want to come inside because they are cold.
5. The teacher told Johnny to stop, but he didn't listen.
6. We are going to the beach.
7. They are not going to the party.
8. You are sitting in the wrong chair.
9. The rabbit was scared, so it ran away.
10. Don't disturb the children; they are asleep.

Answers on page 240.

LESSON 43

NEW WORDS   **je suis**

MEANING   *I am*

PRONUNCIATION TIP: The final *s* in **suis** is silent, so **suis** sounds something like *swee*.

This lesson is special because here we are learning our first French verb. The word **je** is a pronoun that means *I*, and **suis** is the verb which means *am*.

Now that you know your first verb, we can give you exercises that form complete sentences.

EXERCISES:

1. **Je suis ton père.** I am your father
2. **Je suis ta sœur.** I am your sister
3. **Je suis un homme.** I am a man
4. **Je suis ton mari.** I am your husband
5. **Les enfants et les parents.** The children and the parents
6. **Bonjour, ma fille.** Hello, my daughter
7. **Ma femme et des enfants.** My wife and some children
8. **Au revoir, les enfants.** Goodbye, children
9. **Mes enfants, ma femme et ma mère.** my children, my wife, y my mother
10. **L'ami.** The friend

Answers on page 240.

LESSON 44

NEW WORDS   **ne…pas**

MEANING   *not*

PRONUNCIATION TIP: **Ne** sounds something like *nuh*. The *s* in **pas** is silent, so it sounds something like *pah*.

When you negate a verb, you indicate that the action of the verb is not happening. In English it only takes one word to negate a verb, and that is the word *not*. Observe these examples:

> I am your brother.
> I am <u>not</u> your brother.

In the second sentence, we took the word *not* and used it to cancel out the action of the verb. In English, it only takes one word to negate the verb—but in French, it takes two words to say *not*. Observe the following two sentences.

> **Je suis ton frère.**
> **Je <u>ne</u> suis <u>pas</u> ton frère.**

The words **ne** and **pas** work together to negate the verb, adding the word *not* to the English translation of the sentence. In a sentence, the word **ne** comes immediately before the verb and the word **pas** comes immediately after the verb.

EXERCISES:

1. **Je suis.** *I am*
2. **Je ne suis pas.** *I am not you*
3. **Je ne suis pas un enfant.** *I am not your child* *(weird pronunciation)*
4. **Au revoir, mon amie.** *Goodbye my friend*
5. **Des garçons et des filles.** *Some boys and some girls*
6. **L'ami, la mère et le père.** *the friend, the mother, the father "lah'n"*
7. **Bonjour, mes enfants.** *Hello, my children*
8. **Mes parents et une sœur.** *My parents y a sister*
9. **Les femmes et les hommes.** *The women y the men*
10. **L'enfant et tes amis.** *The children y the friends*

Answers on page 240.

LESSON 45

NEW WORDS   **tu es**

MEANING   *you are*

PRONUNCIATION TIP: **Tu** rhymes with *few*. The *s* in **es** is silent, so **es** is pronounced something like *eh*.

Tu is a pronoun that means *you* (singular). **Es** is the verb, which means *are*.

Tu es is singular, so you would use it only when speaking to one person.

Let's talk about elision a bit. In the last lesson, we learned how to negate a verb using **ne...pas**. So, if you want to negate **tu es**, the word **ne** will come right before the word **es**. That will give you this:

Tu n'es pas mon frère *(you are not my brother)*.

Notice the elision between **ne** and **es**, creating the contraction **n'es**.

EXERCISES:

1. **Tu es mon ami.** Your are my friend
2. **Tu n'es pas mon ami.** Your are not my friend
3. **Je suis ton frère.**
4. **Je ne suis pas un homme.** I am not a man
5. **Les enfants et les parents.**
6. **Je suis ta mère.**
7. **Bonjour, mes fils.** Hello, my sons
8. **Un garçon et des filles.**
9. **Au revoir, mon amie.** Goodbye my friend
10. **Je suis ta fille; je ne suis pas ton fils.**

Answers on page 241.

LESSON 46

NEW WORD   **est**

MEANING   *is*

PRONUNCIATION TIP: The *s* and *t* in **est** are silent. So **est** is pronounced something like *eh.*

When you negate the verb **est**, there will be elision between **ne** and **est**, producing the contraction **n'est**.

EXERCISES:

1. **L'homme est mon père.** the man is my father
2. **La femme est ma mère.** the woman is my mother
3. **Ma sœur n'est pas ton amie.** my sister is not your friend
4. **Mon fils est ton ami.** my brother is your friend
5. **L'enfant n'est pas mon frère.** the child is not my brother
6. **Tu es mon amie.** You are my friend
7. **Je ne suis pas une femme.** I am not a woman
8. **Ma femme et les enfants.** my wife and the children
9. **Bonsoir, mes amis.**
10. **Tes sœurs et des filles.** Your sisters and some girls

Answers on page 241.

LESSON 47

NEW WORDS   **il / elle**

MEANING   *he / she*

PRONUNCIATION TIP: **Il** sounds something like the word *eel*, as in *electric eel*. **Elle** rhymes with *bell*.

Il is a pronoun that means *he*. **Elle** is a pronoun that means *she*.

NOTE: Some of the exercises below aren't really the way a native French speaker would talk. But we are giving you these exercises anyway, just so you can get some practice working with these pronouns. So, use these sentences just for practice, and later in the book we will show you more about how to form this kind of sentence.

EXERCISES:

1. **Il n'est pas mon frère.** He is not my brother
2. **Elle est ma sœur.** She is my sister
3. **Il est mon ami.** He is my friend
4. **Elle est ma mère.** She is my mother
5. **Je suis ton père.** I am your father
6. **Tu n'es pas mon frère.** You are not my brother
7. **Un homme, une femme et des enfants.** A man, a woman, and some children
8. **Tes parents et mes amis.** Your parents and my friends
9. **Ma fille et une amie.** A daughter and a friend
10. **Au revoir, mon ami.** goodbye my friend

Answers on page 241.

58

LESSON 48

TITLES AND NAMES

When talking to other people, we use various names and titles to address them. If you know a person well, you will probably use his or her first name. But if it's a person you don't know very well, or someone older than you, you might refer to him or her by a form of address such as *Mr., Mrs.,* or *Miss.* Or, you might say *sir* or *ma'am.*

In English, *Mr.* is a title given to all adult men, whether married or not. *Mrs.* is used for married women, and *Miss* is used for unmarried women.

In French, the word **monsieur** can mean either *Mr.* or *sir* depending on the context. Let's look at a few examples:

> **Bonjour, monsieur** (*Good day, sir*).
> **Bonjour, monsieur Smith** (*Good day, Mr. Smith*).
> **Monsieur Smith est mon ami** (*Mr. Smith is my friend*).
> **Je suis monsieur Smith** (*I am Mr. Smith*).

The word **madame** can mean either *Mrs.* or *ma'am* depending on the context. **Ma** means *my* and **dame** means *lady,* so literally the word **madame** means *my lady.* **Madame** is used to address a married woman or an older, single woman. Let's look at a few examples of how to use the word **madame**:

> **Bonjour, madame** (*Good day, ma'am*).
> **Bonjour, madame Smith** (*Good day, Mrs. Smith*).
> **Madame Smith est mon amie** (*Mrs. Smith is my friend*).
> **Je suis madame Smith** (*I am Mrs. Smith*).

The word **mademoiselle** is in decline, but it is still widely used. It is generally used to address a younger woman or an unmarried woman. It translates into English as *miss.*

EXERCISES:

1. **Bonjour, monsieur.** Goodday, Sir
2. **Bonjour, monsieur Smith.** Goodday, Mr. Smith
3. **Monsieur Smith est mon mari.** Mr. Smith is my husband
4. **Il est mon père.** He is my father
5. **Madame Jones n'est pas ma sœur.** Mrs. Jones is not my sister
6. **Au revoir, mademoiselle.** Goodbye, miss
7. **Elle est la fille.** She is the daughter
8. **Tu es ma femme.** You are my wife
9. **Je suis une fille.** I am a girl
10. **Mes parents et tes enfants.** My parents and your children

Answers on page 242.

EXPRESSIONS FRANÇAISES

You have probably heard the famous expression *I think, therefore I am*. That's the English translation of the Latin phrase **cogito ergo sum**. But did you know that this thought was written in French before it was written in Latin?

This idea comes from the great French philosopher René Descartes. In French, it's **je pense, donc je suis**. You already know the words **je** and **suis**. Can you figure out the rest on your own?

LESSON 49

NEW WORDS   **nous sommes**

MEANING   *we are*

PRONUNCIATION TIP: **Nous** sounds vaguely similar to the word *new*, and **sommes** sounds somewhat like the word *some*.

Nous is the pronoun here, and it means *we*. **Sommes** is the verb, which means *are*.

EXERCISES:

1. **Nous sommes tes parents.** We are your parents
2. **Monsieur Jones est mon frère.** Mr. Jones is my brother
3. **Il est monsieur Smith.** He is Mr. Smith
4. **Bonjour, madame.** Hello, Madame
5. **Elle n'est pas madame Smith; elle est madame Jones.** She is not Mrs. Smith, She is Mrs. Jones
6. **Tu es mon frère.** You are my brother
7. **Je ne suis pas ton fils.** I am not your son
8. **Les femmes et des enfants.** The women and some children
9. **L'ami.** the friend
10. **Des amis et mes sœurs.** Some friends and my sister

Answers on page 242.

61

LESSON 50

NEW WORDS   **vous êtes**

MEANING   *you are (plural)*

PRONUNCIATION TIP: By itself, **vous** sounds like *voo* because the *s* is silent. But with the word **êtes**, there is a liaison, so **vous êtes** sounds something like *voo-zette*.

Vous is a pronoun that means *you*, but plural. **Êtes** is the verb, and it means *are*.

You already know that **tu es** means *you are*. We use **tu es** when speaking to one person. **Vous êtes** also means *you are*, but with one important difference: **vous êtes** is plural. The English word *you* can refer to one person or more than one person. But other languages, such as French and Spanish, have a separate word for singular *you* and for plural *you*.

Sometimes English speakers use expressions such as *you all*, *you guys*, or *you people* to try to make it clear that we are talking to more than one person. In the southeastern United States, we often use the contraction *y'all* to address more than one person (never just one). *Y'all* is simply a contraction of the words *you* and *all*. *Y'all* rhymes with *hall*, *ball*, and *fall*. So, in the answer key, **vous êtes** will be translated as *y'all are*, to help you distinguish plural *you* from singular *you*. If you are from the southeastern United States, using this word will be easy for you. If not, y'all will get used to it after using it a few times. In any case, just try to have fun with it.

IMPORTANT NOTE

Although **vous** is plural, it can also be used when you are speaking to one person. When you use **vous** to address one person, it is considered a more formal way to speak. This type of speech would be appropriate if you do not know the person you are speaking with very well. Of course, when speaking to friends or family, you can always use **tu**.

When you see the word **vous** in the exercises, you will need to use context to help yourself determine if **vous** is second person plural or a formal-sounding second person singular.

62

Let's look at a few examples to help you think about the context of **vous** and how it can be used.

> **Vous êtes le président** *(You are the president).*

In this example, it is clear that **vous** is singular because the word **président** is singular. (For you grammatical types, notice that when you use **vous** as a formal singular, it draws a singular predicate).

Here's another example:

> **Vous êtes mes amis** *(Y'all are my friends).*

In this example, it is clear that **vous** is plural because **mes** and **amis** are both plural. (If **vous** were singular here, it would say **vous êtes mon ami**, with a singular **mon** and a singular **ami**).

Here's a slightly tougher one, so put on your thinking cap. It uses a new word, **ici**, which means *here*. **Ici** sounds something like *ee-see*.

> **Vous êtes ici** *(You are here).*

In this example, is **vous** singular or plural? Well, the sentence doesn't give us enough context to know for sure, so **vous** could be either singular or plural.

EXERCISES:

1. **Vous êtes mes amis.** You are my friend
2. **Vous êtes mes enfants.** You are my children
3. **Vous êtes madame Smith.** You are Mrs. Smith
4. **Bonne nuit, mon ami.** Goodnight, mon ami
5. **Il est mon papa.** He is my Dad
6. **Monsieur Smith est mon père.** Mr. Smith is my father
7. **Au revoir, madame Jones.** Goodbye, Mrs. Jones
8. **Nous ne sommes pas tes filles.** We are not your daughter
9. **Tu n'es pas mon frère.** You are not my brother
10. **Elle est mon amie.** She is my friend

Answers on page 242.

LESSON 51

NEW WORDS   **ils / elles**

MEANING   *they*

PRONUNCIATION TIP: In each of these words, the *s* is silent—unless the next word starts with a vowel. Then, there will be a liaison with the next word.

Ils is the plural form of the masculine pronoun **il**. And likewise, **elles** is the plural form of the feminine pronoun **elle**. **Ils** and **elles** both mean *they*.

If you want to say *they* (referring to a group of males), you would use the word **ils**. If you want to say *they* (referring to a group of females only), you would use **elles**. And, as we explained way back in lesson 30, if the group of people contains both males and females, you would use **ils**, the masculine form.

LESSON 52

NEW WORD   **sont**

MEANING   *are*

PRONUNCIATION TIP: The word **sont** ends with a nasal sound (the *t* is silent).

In the last lesson, you learned about the pronouns **ils** and **elles**. Now you can use them with the verb **sont**, the new word for this lesson, which means *are*.

EXERCISES:

1. **Elles sont mes sœurs.** They are my sisters
2. **Ils sont tes amis.** They are my your friends
3. **Elles ne sont pas mes filles.** They are not my daughter
4. **Vous êtes mes amies.** You are my friends
5. **Nous sommes tes amis.** We are your friends
6. **Bonjour, monsieur Jones.** Hello, Mr Jones
7. **Elle est ma mère.** She is my mother.
8. **Tu es un garçon.** You are a boy.
9. **Je ne suis pas un enfant.** I am not a child.
10. **Les hommes et des femmes.** The men and some women

Answers on page 243.

LESSON 53

MEMORIZATION

Let's put all the pronouns and verbs you know into a chart to help you remember them.

Être

je suis	nous sommes
tu es	vous êtes
il/elle est	ils/elles sont

When studying any language, it is very beneficial to memorize groups of verbs such as the one you see here. Of course, the most common way to memorize these verbs is simply to repeat them over and over. This might be a little boring, but you can make this necessary repetition more fun by making a song or a game out of it, especially if children are involved.

LESSON 54

PERSON

We have already covered singular and plural, so now let's talk about another quality that verbs have. In French, verbs (with help from their pronouns) tell not only what action is taking place, but also who is performing the action. Verbs can be in the first person, second person, or third person.

❑ Verbs that refer to *I* or *we* are first person (referring to the person who is speaking).

❑ Verbs that refer to *you*, either singular or plural, are second person (referring to the person or people to whom the speaker is speaking). In this book we will use *y'all* for the second person plural to help distinguish it from the second person singular.

❑ Verbs that refer to *he, she, it*, or *they* are third person (referring to the person, thing, people, or things being spoken about).

The following chart should help illustrate this concept:

	SINGULAR	PLURAL
FIRST PERSON	**I**	**we**
SECOND PERSON	**you**	**you** *y'all*
THIRD PERSON	**he, she, it**	**they**

In the exercises on the next page, determine what the subject of each sentence is. Then, determine if the subject is first person, second person, or third person. Finally, determine whether it is singular or plural.

EXERCISES:

1st, singular 1. I am tired.

2nd, either 2. You are really good at chess.

3rd, singular 3. She passed the test.

1st, plural 4. We are going to school.

2nd, plural 5. Y'all have an expensive car.

3rd, plural 6. They eat breakfast at Aunt Martha's house every Saturday.

3rd, singular 7. He is a trombone player.

3rd, singular 8. It is a history book.

2nd, plural 9. Y'all really know how to throw a party.

3rd, plural 10. The flowers in your garden are very colorful.

Answers on page 243.

LESSON 55

REVIEW

Now let's put all the French verbs you know into a chart, along with their accompanying pronouns.

ÊTRA (TO BE) [handwritten]

	SINGULAR	PLURAL
FIRST PERSON	*I* je suis	*we* nous sommes
SECOND PERSON	*You* tu es	*Y'all* vous êtes
THIRD PERSON	*He, she, it* il/elle est	*they* ils/elles sont

on [handwritten]

As you memorize this chart, don't just memorize the French words—also think about what each word means.

LESSON 56

NEW WORD   **chien**

MEANING   *dog*

PRONUNCIATION TIP: **Chien** sounds something like *shee-eh*.

EXERCISES:

1. **Mon fils et des chiens.** My son and some dogs
2. **Le chien est mon ami.** The dog is my friend
3. **Les chiens sont mes amis.** The dogs are my friends
4. **Monsieur Smith n'est pas mon père.** Mr. Smith is not my father
5. **Elles sont mes sœurs.** They are my sisters
6. **Vous êtes mes sœurs.** You are my sisters
7. **Nous ne sommes pas tes amis—nous sommes tes parents.** We are not your friends, we are your parent
8. **Ta sœur est mon amie.** Your sister is my friend
9. **Monsieur et madame Jones sont mes parents.** Mr. and Mrs. Jones are my parents
10. **Tu es mon amie.** You are my friend

Answers on page 243.

70

LESSON 57

PRONUNCIATION TIP: These numbers don't sound anything like they look—
so be sure to listen carefully to the pronunciation recordings.

In this lesson, let's try to memorize the numbers zero through six in French. Here
is a chart to help you learn these numbers.

English	French
zero	**zéro**
one	**un / une**
two	**deux**
three	**trois**
four	**quatre**
five	**cinq**
six	**six**

(handwritten notes beside chart: "uah", "dœ", "twa", "cat", "sank", "sees")

Notice that the words for the number *one* are **un** and **une**, which are the singular
indefinite articles. Therefore, when you use the masculine indefinite article and
say **un homme**, you are literally saying *one man*. And likewise, when you use the
feminine indefinite article and say **une femme**, you are literally saying *one woman*.
So, in French there is no difference between the number *one* and the indefinite
article.

When you see a number, and then the next word starts with a vowel, watch out for
possible liaisons and also enchaînement. We will help you out with these issues in
the commentary recordings.

EXERCISES:

1. **Un homme.**
2. **Une sœur.**

3. **356-0142 (trois cinq six zéro un quatre deux).**
4. **Deux garçons et cinq femmes.** *2 boys and 5 woman*
5. **La fille, des garçons et six chiens.** *The girl, some boys, and 6 dogs*
6. **Elles sont mes filles.** *The are my daughters*
7. **Nous ne sommes pas tes parents.** *We're not your parent*
8. **Vous êtes mes frères.** *You are my brothers*
9. **Il est mon père.** *He is my father*
10. **Je suis ton enfant.** *I am your child*

Answers on page 244.

EXPRESSIONS FRANÇAISES

Have you ever heard someone make a statement like this?

"I really like this house. It has that certain **je ne sais quoi.**"

This expression means *I don't know what.* People use it sometimes when they are trying to find the right words to describe something, but can't quite put their finger on it.

You already know what **je** means. The word **ne** means *not.* **Sais** means *know,* and **quoi** means *what.* Put it all together, and you get **je ne sais quoi,** which means *I don't know what.*

72

[handwritten top right: ⚹ eu-uh]

LESSON 58

NUMBERS, CONTINUED

In this lesson, let's try to memorize the numbers seven through twelve in French.

English	French	
seven	**sept**	*"set"*
eight	**huit**	*"weet"*
nine	**neuf**	*nuhf*
ten	**dix**	*"dix" diss*
eleven	**onze**	*"onz"*
twelve	**douze**	*"dooz"*

As we mentioned before, remember to be on the lookout for liaisons and enchaînement.

Here are some exercises to help you learn to translate these numbers.

EXERCISES:

1. **Sept amis.** *7 friends*
2. **Neuf enfants.** *9 children*
3. **790-8415 (sept neuf zéro huit quatre un cinq).** *auh sank*
4. **Dix chiens et douze enfants.** *10 dogs & 12 children*
5. **Onze filles et des garçons.** *11 daughters & some boys*
6. **Je suis ta sœur et vous êtes mes frères.** *I am your sister & you are my brothers*
7. **Tu es mon amie.** *You are my friend (female)*
8. **Madame Smith n'est pas ma sœur.** *Mrs. Smith is not my sister*
9. **Ils ne sont pas mes enfants.**
10. **Nous sommes les parents et ils sont les enfants.**

Answers on page 244.

73

LESSON 59

NEW WORD   **chat**

MEANING   *cat*

PRONUNCIATION TIP: **Chat** sounds something like *shah*.

EXERCISES:

1. **Deux chats et quatre chiens.** *shah* *"cat"* 2 cats and four dogs
2. **Trois frères et cinq sœurs.** 3 brothers and 5 sisters
3. **Six chats et neuf chiens.** *nurf* 6 cats and 9 dogs
4. **Sept garçons et dix filles.** *Set* 7 boys and 10 girls
5. **Mon chat est mon ami.** *Mes* chat is my friend (m)
6. **Mes chats sont mes amis.** my cats are my friends
7. **Tu es mon amie.** You are my friend (F)
8. **Nous ne sommes pas sœurs.** We are not sisters
9. **Vous êtes mes amies.** You are my friends
10. **Elle est mon amie.** She is my friend (F)

Answers on page 244.

LESSON 60

NEW WORD   **j'ai**

MEANING   *I have*

PRONUNCIATION TIP: Think of the word *vision*. The *s* in vision has sort of a *zh* sound to it. That's the sound that starts **j'ai**. Therefore, **j'ai** sounds something like *zhay*.

J'ai is our first action verb in French. All the verbs you have learned so far have been verbs of being or existing (in English, we call these verbs *linking verbs*). But now that we know how to say **j'ai**, hopefully we can make more interesting sentences.

As you may have noticed, **j'ai** has an apostrophe in it. That means it contains an elision. **J'ai** is actually made up of two words:

je ai

Je, as you already know, means *I*. And **ai** is the verb which means *have*. When you put **je** and **ai** together, there is elision between them, creating this contraction:

j'ai   " *Juy* "

And if you negate **j'ai**, there will be elision between **ne** and **ai**, giving you this:

je n'ai pas

EXERCISES:

1. **J'ai trois chiens.**   I have 3 dogs
2. **J'ai deux chats.**   I have 2 cat
3. **J'ai huit chats et dix chiens.**   *shaa*   I have 8 cats and 10 dogs
4. **J'ai des chiens.**   I have some dogs
5. **Ta sœur est ma sœur.**   Your sister is may sister

75

6. **Ils sont mes amis.** *They are my friends*
7. **J'ai un fils et neuf filles.** *I have a son and 9 daughters*
8. **Je suis ta mère.** *I am your mother*
9. **Vous êtes mes amies.** *You are my friends (F)*
10. **Monsieur Smith est mon ami.** *Mr. Smith is my friend*

Answers on page 245.

LESSON 61

MORE ABOUT DES

By this point in the book, you might be thinking that the plural indefinite article **des** always translates into English as the word *some*. But when you translate from French to English, you don't always need to translate **des** as *some*—in fact, you may not need to translate **des** at all. Here's an example to show you what we mean.

Nous avons des chats.

Here are two ways you could translate that sentence into English:

We have some cats.
We have cats.

This demonstrates a difference between French and English. In the French example sentence, the word **des** is required according to the rules of French grammar—in other words, you cannot leave it out. But in the English translation, we could either put in or leave out the corresponding word *some*. It is not required. Both English translations mean the same thing, and both are grammatically correct.

Here's another example to practice with:

Ils ont des chiens.

Here are two ways you could translate that sentence into English:

They have some dogs.
They have dogs.

Again, as you translate this French sentence into English, you could choose to put in or leave out the word *some*. Both translations mean the same thing, and both are grammatically correct.

Take a few moments to practice with the examples given above until you understand that **des** doesn't necessarily translate into anything in English.

"au" = o

LESSON 62

NEW WORD   **aussi**

MEANING   *also*

PRONUNCIATION TIP: **Aussi** sounds vaguely like *oh-see.*

EXERCISES:

1. **J'ai dix chiens et aussi un chat.** I have 10 dog and also a cat
2. **J'ai quatre frères. J'ai aussi trois sœurs.** I have 4 brothers. I also have 3 sisters
3. **J'ai douze chats. J'ai aussi des chiens.** I have 12 cats. I also have some dogs
4. **Mon chien est mon ami.** My dog is my friend
5. **Bonjour, madame—je suis monsieur Jones.** Hello, Mrs. — I am Mr. Jones
6. **J'ai une sœur.** I have a sister
7. **Elle est ma mère.** She is my mother
8. **Nous sommes tes parents.** We are your parents
9. **Je suis une femme et tu es un homme.** I am a woman and you are a man
10. **Vous êtes madame Smith.** You are Mrs. Smith

Answers on page 245.

LESSON 63

NEW WORD **livre**

MEANING *book*

Livre is a masculine noun.

EXERCISES:

1. **J'ai les livres.** I have the books
2. **Je n'ai pas cinq livres.** I do not have 5 books
3. **J'ai sept chats et aussi neuf chiens.** I have 7 cats and also 9 dogs
4. **J'ai des chats. J'ai aussi un chien.** I have some cats. I have also a dog
5. **Mon chat est mon ami.** My cat is my friend
6. **Ils sont mes frères.** They are my brothers
7. **Ma fille est ton amie.** My daughter is your friend
8. **Vous êtes madame Jones.** Your are Mrs. Jones
9. **Je suis ta sœur.** I am your sister
10. **Je suis l'homme.** I am the man

Answers on page 245.

LESSON 64

NEW WORD  **voiture**

MEANING   *car*

PRONUNCIATION TIP: **Voiture** sounds something like *vwah-tew-r.*

Voiture is a feminine noun, so it will need a feminine article like **la** or **une.** Nouns that end in *-ure* are usually feminine.

EXERCISES:

1. **Je n'ai pas trois voitures.** I dont have three cars
2. **J'ai des livres.** I have some books
3. **J'ai quatre voitures.** I have 4 cars
4. **J'ai huit chats. J'ai aussi deux chiens.** I have 8 cats. I also have 2 dogs
5. **J'ai une voiture.** I have a car
6. **Je suis un homme.** I am a man
7. **Tu n'es pas mon chien—tu es mon chat.** You are not my dog — you are my cat
8. **Les filles sont mes amies.** The girls are my friend
9. **J'ai trois livres.** I have 3 books
10. **J'ai une sœur.** I have a sister

Answers on page 246.

LESSON 65

- used for nouns you can count

ARTICLES AND QUANTITY

A while ago we studied the difference between the definite article and the indefinite article. Let's review those articles again.

luh

	SINGULAR	PLURAL
DEFINITE ARTICLE	the (**le, la**)	the (**les**) "*le*"
INDEFINITE ARTICLE	a, an (**un, une**)	some (**des**) "*duh*"

1

To pick the right article for a noun, you need to determine if the noun is singular or plural. It's a simple process to figure out if something is singular or plural—you just count it. If there is only one of something, it is singular. If there is more than one of something, it is plural. One broom is singular. Two brooms are plural. If you can count it, you can figure it out.

But what about things that you cannot count? If you can't count it, how do you know if it is singular or plural? Consider the following sentence:

Please give me some coffee.

In this case, is *coffee* singular or plural? Can you count coffee? You could count cups of coffee, but how do you count the coffee itself? Here's another sentence to consider:

I have some rice.

The word *rice* seems to be singular, but when you introduce it with the word *some* it makes it sound sort of plural. I suppose you could count the grains of rice, but that's not very practical. So, is it singular or plural?

Here's the point. In French, if there is something you cannot count, you cannot use the definite articles and indefinite articles you would normally use. Instead there is a third kind of article you must use with words like these, and we will learn about it in the next lesson.

LESSON 66

THE PARTITIVE ARTICLE

In the last lesson we learned that in French there is a special kind of article that we use with things that cannot be counted. This kind of article is called the *partitive article*. It is called the partitive article because it shows that you are referring to just a part of a larger whole.

As we mentioned a moment ago, some things are not really singular or plural, such as coffee or rice (as you may have noticed, this is common with food-related words). For substances like these, which cannot be counted, we must use the partitive article. Consider the following sentence:

I have some rice.

In English, we say the word *some* to indicate that we have a certain unknown quantity of something like rice. In English, you could even leave out the word *some* and say this:

I have rice.

Now there is no introductory word at all—there is no *the, a, an,* or *some.* In English, this is allowed. It still expresses the idea that you have an undefined, unknown quantity of rice. In French, however, you can't make a sentence with this exact wording. In other words, you can't say this:

J'ai riz.

That would be incorrect. Instead, if you have an unknown, undefined quantity of something you *must* use the partitive article, like this:

J'ai du riz (*I have some rice* OR *I have rice*).

In this sentence the word **du** is the partitive article. **Riz** is a masculine noun which means *rice,* and **du** is the masculine singular partitive article.

Du is really a combination of the two words **de** and **le. De** means *of,* and **le** means *the.* When you say **j'ai du café,** literally you are saying *I have of the coffee.* But

82

de and **le** combine to form the word **du** leaving the sentence **j'ai du café** which translates into English as *I have some coffee.*

Du is masculine—but what if you have a food-related noun that is feminine, like the word **dinde** which means *turkey*?

> **J'ai de la dinde** *(I have some turkey* OR *I have turkey).*

The feminine singular partitive article is comprised of two words, **de** and **la**. But the words **de** and **la** do not combine to form a new, shorter word in the same way that **de** and **le** combine to form **du**. Therefore, this feminine partitive is a two-word article.

Also, if a partitive article comes before a noun which starts with a vowel, the spelling of the partitive article changes due to elision. This happens regardless of whether the noun is masculine or feminine. In order to practice this, we need a French noun that starts with a vowel. Let's use the French word for *money*, which is **argent**. Then we can say things like this:

> **J'ai de l'argent** *(I have some money* OR *I have money).*

Since the word **argent** starts with a vowel, and we are using the partitive article with it, the partitive article will keep its two-word form but there will be elision between the partitive and the noun it introduces. This is true whether the noun is masculine or feminine (**argent** happens to be masculine).

Here are the partitive articles in a handy chart.

Masculine Partitive Article	**du** (**de l'** before a vowel)
Feminine Partitive Article	**de la** (**de l'** before a vowel)

In the following exercises, get some practice working with the partitive article. Keep in mind that the English translation may not always need the word *some.*

EXERCISES:

1. **J'ai du riz.** *I have some riz*
2. **J'ai de la dinde.** *I have some turkey*
3. **J'ai de l'argent.** *I have some money*
4. **Je suis un chat.** *I am a cat*
5. **J'ai des chats. J'ai aussi un chien.** *I have cats, I also have a dog.*
6. **J'ai des livres.** *I have books*
7. **J'ai trois voitures.** *I have 3 cars*
8. **Tes sœurs sont mes amies.** *Your sisters are my friend*
9. **Ils ont des chiens.** *they have dogs*
10. **Vous êtes mes parents.** *You are my parents*

Answers on page 246.

EXPRESSIONS FRANÇAISES

When the realities of life strike, people sometimes say the expression **c'est la vie**.

C'est is a contraction of two words: **ce** and **est**. **Ce** means *this/that/it*, and **est**, as you already know, means *is*. **C'est**, therefore, can mean *this is*, *that is*, or *it is*.

La means *the*, and the last word in this expression, **vie**, means *life*. So, the expression **c'est la vie** means *that's life*. We use the definite article **la** here because we are speaking about life in general. This illustrates a difference between French and English—in French, the definite article is required before nouns much more often than they are in English.

LESSON 67

de
des
du

NEW WORD **nourriture**

MEANING *food*

Nourriture, our new word for this lesson, is feminine (nouns that end in *-ure* are usually feminine). Therefore, if you use the partitive article with it, it would look like this: **de la nourriture**.

EXERCISES:

1. **J'ai de la nourriture.** I have food
2. **J'ai de l'argent.** I have money
3. **J'ai de la dinde.** I have turkey
4. **J'ai du riz.** I have rice
5. **J'ai deux voitures.** I have 2 cars
6. **J'ai cinq livres.** I have 5 books
7. **J'ai des frères et aussi des sœurs.** I have brothers and also sisters
8. **Nous sommes sœurs.** We are sisters.
9. **Tu es mon ami.** You are my friend
10. **Elle est ma femme.** She is my wife

Answers on page 246.

85

LESSON 68

NEW WORDS **dollar / euro / franc**

MEANING *dollar / euro / franc*

All three of our new words for this lesson are masculine. The word **dollar** can refer to U.S. dollars or dollars in other countries where the currency is called a dollar (Canada or Australia, for example). The **euro** is the currency used in many countries throughout Europe, including France. Before adopting the **euro**, France used the **franc**. Switzerland is a French-speaking country that still uses its own currency, the Swiss franc.

EXERCISES:

1. **J'ai un dollar.** I have a dollar
2. **J'ai dix euros et neuf francs.** I have 10 euros and 9 francs
3. **J'ai quatre francs et aussi un euro.** I have 4 francs and also a euro
4. **J'ai de l'argent... j'ai cinq euros et onze dollars.** I have money,... I have 5 euros and 11 dollars
5. **J'ai sept chats. J'ai aussi huit chiens.** I have 7 cats: I also have 8 dogs
6. **J'ai de la dinde et du riz.** I have turkey and rice
7. **Vous êtes monsieur Jones.** You are Mr. Jones.
8. **Je n'ai pas mon livre.** I do not have my book
9. **J'ai ma voiture.** I have my car.
10. **Je ne suis pas un enfant.** I am not a child.

Answers on page 247.

LESSON 69

NEW WORDS **tu as**

MEANING *you have*

PRONUNCIATION TIP: The *s* in **as** is silent.

If you negate **tu as**, there will be elision between **ne** and **as**, which would produce this: **tu n'as pas**.

This chart should come in handy as we learn all the different forms of **j'ai**.

AVOIR (TO HAVE)

	SINGULAR	PLURAL
FIRST PERSON	j'ai	
SECOND PERSON	tu as	
THIRD PERSON		

EXERCISES:

1. **Tu as cinq euros.** You have 5 euros
2. **Tu as de l'argent.** *shoo*
3. **Tu as du riz et j'ai de la dinde.** *and* You have rice and I have turkey
4. **Je n'ai pas ton argent.** I do not have your money
5. **Tu n'es pas une mère.** You are not a mother
6. **Tu as deux chats.** You have two cats
7. **Tu as huit euros et trois dollars.** You have 8 euros and 3 dollars
8. **Il n'est pas mon père.** He is not my father
9. **Tu as de la nourriture.** You have some food
10. **Tu es mon amie…nous sommes amies.** You are my friend (F)… we are friends

Answers on page 247.

LESSON 70

NEW WORDS   **il / elle a**

MEANING   *he / she has*

If you negate **il a** or **elle a**, with elision it would look like **il n'a pas** and **elle n'a pas**.

The chart is now halfway full.

	SINGULAR	PLURAL
FIRST PERSON	**j'ai**	
SECOND PERSON	**tu as**	
THIRD PERSON	**il/elle a**	

EXERCISES:

1. **Il a mon argent.** He has my money
2. **Elle a des livres.** She has some books
3. **Mon fils a de l'argent.** My son has some money
4. **Il n'a pas trois dollars.** He does not have 3 $
5. **Il a neuf enfants—deux fils et aussi sept filles.** He has 9 children - 2 sons and also 7 daughters
6. **Je suis ton ami.** I am your friend
7. **Tu as dix sœurs et aussi un frère.** You have 10 sisters and also a brother
8. **Ma fille a ma voiture.** My daughter has my car
9. **Ils sont mes amis et vous êtes mes frères.** They are my friends, and you are my brothers.
10. **Tu as de la dinde et du riz.** You have Turkey and rice

Answers on page 247.

LESSON 71

NEW WORD **mais** _e_ "me"

MEANING _but_

PRONUNCIATION TIP: The _s_ in **mais** is silent.

EXERCISES:

1. **J'ai un chien, mais tu as un chat.** I have a dog, but you have a cat
2. **Tu n'as pas ton chat, mais tu as ton chien.** You do not have your cat, but you have your dog.
3. **Mon chat est mon ami, mais ton chien est ton ami.** my cat is my friend, but your dog is your friend
4. **Mon frère a mon argent.** my brother has my money
5. **J'ai quatre chiens. J'ai aussi cinq chats.** I have 4 dogs. I also have 5 cats.
6. **Madame Smith a mes livres.** mrs. smith has my books
7. **Nous sommes amies, mais ils ne sont pas mes amis.** We are friends, but they are not my friends
8. **Elle a de la nourriture.** she has some food.
9. **Tu n'as pas six euros.** You do not have 6 euros
10. **J'ai du riz.** I have some rice

Answers on page 248.

89

LESSON 72

nous avons

MEANING *we have*

PRONUNCIATION TIP: Just by itself, the word **nous** has a silent *s*. But when it comes before the word **avons**, there will be a liaison between **nous** and **avons**, and it will sound something like *new-zavoh*.

If you negate **nous avons**, there will be elision between **ne** and **avons**, giving you this:

nous n'avons pas

	SINGULAR	PLURAL
FIRST PERSON	**j'ai**	**nous avons**
SECOND PERSON	**tu as**	
THIRD PERSON	**il/elle a**	

EXERCISES:

1. **Nous avons des amis.** We have some friends
2. **Nous n'avons pas trois sœurs.** We do not have 3 sisters
3. **Tu as un dollar. J'ai aussi un dollar.** You have one dollar. I also have one dollar.
4. **Elle n'a pas ma voiture.** She does not have my car.
5. **Je n'ai pas ton argent.** I do not have your money
6. **Les filles sont mes sœurs et les garçons sont mes frères.** The girls are my sisters and the boys are my brothers
7. **Elle a cinq fils et aussi six filles.** She has 5 sons and also 6 daughters
8. **Nous avons de la dinde.** We have some turkey
9. **Mon père a la voiture.** My father has the car
10. **Tu es mon ami, mais il est mon frère.** You are my friend, but he is my father.

Answers on page 248.

LESSON 73

NEW WORDS   **vous avez**

MEANING   *y'all have* (OR, using formal speech) *you have*

PRONUNCIATION TIP: Watch out for the liaison between **vous** and **avez**.

Since **vous** can be both plural and singular, you must determine from the context of the sentence whether **vous** is being used as a singular pronoun or as a plural pronoun. And if you negate **vous avez**, there will be elision between **ne** and **avez**, giving you this:

    vous n'avez pas

The chart is almost full—please try to contain your excitement.

	SINGULAR	PLURAL
FIRST PERSON	**j'ai**	**nous avons**
SECOND PERSON	**tu as**	**vous avez**
THIRD PERSON	**il/elle a**	

Sometimes, a sentence doesn't provide enough context to determine whether **vous** is intended to be plural or a formal-sounding singular. In these cases, the answer key will translate the exercise both ways to facilitate your learning.

EXERCISES:

1. **Vous avez mes livres.** Ya'll have my books
2. **Vous avez du riz.** Ya'll have some rice
3. **Nous avons ma voiture.** we have my car
4. **Il a de l'argent.** he has some money

91

5. **Tu n'as pas dix euros.** *You do not have 10 euros*

6. **Tu as sept sœurs, mais j'ai douze sœurs et un frère.** *You have 7 sisters but I have 12 sisters and a brothers*

7. **Ma sœur a ma voiture.** *My sister has my car*

8. **Ils sont mes enfants.** *They are my children*

9. **Les enfants sont tes frères et tes sœurs.** *The children are your brothers and your sisters*

10. **Elle n'est pas mon amie.** *She is not my friend.*

Answers on page 248.

LESSON 74

NEW WORDS   **ils / elles ont**

MEANING   *they have*

PRONUNCIATION TIP: Watch for the liaison between **ils** and **ont**, and also between **elles** and **ont**.

If you negate **ils ont** or **elles ont**, there will be elision between **ne** and **ont**, giving you this:

ils n'ont pas
elles n'ont pas

Our chart is now full!

	SINGULAR	PLURAL
FIRST PERSON	**j'ai**	*we have* **nous avons**
SECOND PERSON	**tu as**	**vous avez**
THIRD PERSON	**il/elle a**	**ils/elles ont**

EXERCISES:

1. **Ils ont mon argent !** *They have my money!*
2. **Elles n'ont pas trois voitures—elles ont deux voitures.** *They (F) do not have 3 cars— they F have 2 cars*
3. **Ils ont trois enfants, mais nous avons deux enfants.** *they have 3 children but we have 2 children*
4. **Madame Jones, vous n'êtes pas ma mère.** *Mrs. Jones, you are not my brother.*
5. **J'ai quatre chats et aussi des chiens.** *I have 4 cats and also some dogs*
6. **Les garçons sont mes fils.** *the boys are my sons*
7. **Vous avez de l'argent.** *Ya'll have some money*
8. **Monsieur Smith a six frères.** *mr Smith has 6 brothers*
9. **Tu as des amis.** *You are my friends*
10. **Elle a dix euros.** *She has 10 euros*

Answers on page 249.

LESSON 75

REVIEW

We now know all the present tense forms of **je suis** and **j'ai**. Let's review them now. Here is the chart for **je suis**:

ETRA (TO BE)

	SINGULAR	PLURAL
FIRST PERSON	je suis	nous sommes
SECOND PERSON	tu es	vous êtes
THIRD PERSON	il/elle est	ils/elles sont

You should make every effort to memorize these forms. Chant them. Sing them. Do whatever helps you to memorize the different verb forms.

Here is the chart for **j'ai**:

AVOIT (TO HAVE)

	SINGULAR	PLURAL
FIRST PERSON	j'ai	nous avons
SECOND PERSON	tu as	vous avez
THIRD PERSON	il/elle a	ils/elles ont

As you repeat or recite these verb forms, don't just memorize the words—also try to think of what each word means as you say it.

94

LESSON 76

I DON'T HAVE ANY!

A few lessons ago, we learned about the partitive article. We use the partitive article with nouns that cannot be counted. Here are some of the things we learned how to say:

J'ai du riz *(I have some rice* OR *I have rice).*
Nous avons de la dinde *(We have some turkey* OR *We have turkey).*
Il a de l'argent *(He has some money* OR *He has money).*

At this point, we have had some good practice working with the partitive article. We know how to say that we have some of something—but how would we say the opposite of that? In other words, how do we say that we do *not* have some of something? To make this kind of statement in English, we usually use the word *any*, like this:

I don't have any rice.
We don't have any turkey.
He doesn't have any money.

To make this kind of statement in French, as you might expect, you must negate the verb using **ne...pas**. But the partitive article changes, too. In a negative construction, in place of **du, de la**, or **de l'**, we use the word **de**. Observe the following examples:

Je n'ai pas de riz *(I do not have any rice* OR *I do not have rice).*
Nous n'avons pas de dinde *(We do not have any turkey* OR *We do not have turkey).*

If the next word starts with a vowel, there will be elision, like this:

Il n'a pas d'argent *(He does not have any money* OR *He does not have money).*

We use this same kind of sentence structure not only to say that we don't have uncountable things, like foods, but countable things, too. Let's say, for instance, that you want to say *I do not have a cat.* To say this, you would negate the verb, then put the word **de**, and then put the noun that you don't have, like this:

95

Je n'ai pas de chat *(I do not have a cat).*

And the sentence structure is the same if you want to say that you don't have any of some plural item, like this:

Je n'ai pas de chats *(I do not have any cats* OR *I do not have cats).*

This rule does not apply to statements in which the noun is being introduced by a definite article. Let's say, for instance, that you want to tell someone that you have a specific cat, such as Fluffy, Snowflake, or Scooter. Then you might say something like this:

J'ai le chat *(I have the cat).*

In that case, since you are talking about a specific cat, when you negate the statement, you will keep the definite article.

Je n'ai pas <u>le</u> chat *(I do not have the cat).*

So, in closing, remember this: whether the noun you don't have is singular, plural, countable, uncountable, masculine, or feminine, use the word **de** before it to say that you don't have it. But if it has a definite article in front of it, don't use **de** and let the noun keep its definite article.

EXERCISES:

1. **J'ai du riz.** I have rice.
2. **Je n'ai pas de riz.** I do not have rice.
3. **Tu as de l'argent.** You have some money
4. **Tu n'as pas d'argent.** You do not have money
5. **Nous n'avons pas d'enfants.** We do not have children
6. **Vous avez huit enfants, mais ils n'ont pas d'enfants.** You all have 8 children but they do not have children
7. **Je n'ai pas de voiture.** I have no car.
8. **Je n'ai pas <u>la</u> voiture.** I do not have the car
9. **Ma sœur a dix euros. Elle a aussi cinq dollars.** My sister has 10 euros. She also has 5 dollars
10. **Nous n'avons pas de nourriture.** We don't have food.

Answers on page 249.

LESSON 77

NEW WORDS   **son / sa**

MEANING   *his, her*

You already know how to say *my* and *your*, but in this lesson you are going to learn how to say *his* and *her*. For this, we use the words **son** and **sa**. **Son** and **sa** function just like **mon/ma** and **ton/ta**. **Son** is masculine and **sa** is feminine.

If we put **mon/ma**, **ton/ta**, and **son/sa** into a chart, it would look like this.

similar to Spanish

	SINGULAR	PLURAL
FIRST PERSON	**mon/ma/mes**	
SECOND PERSON	**ton/ta/tes**	
THIRD PERSON	**son/sa/ses**	

You see, **mon/ma** *(my)* makes reference to the speaker, so these words are first person. **Ton/ta** *(your)* makes reference to the person being spoken to, so these words are second person. And **son/sa**, our new words for this lesson, refer to the person being spoken about, so these words are third person.

As you examine the chart, you will notice that these forms are listed in the singular column. These forms are singular from the perspective of the number of people possessing something. In other words, these are singular in the sense that they show that something belongs to only one person (me, you, him, or her). In the next lesson, we will begin to learn how to say that something belongs to more than one person—that is, the French words for *our* and *their*. In the chart you see above, words like those would go in the right-hand (plural) column.

Remember, these words agree in gender with the thing being possessed, *not* with the gender of the person possessing it. This is different from English. In English, the words *his* and *her* agree with gender of the person possessing the thing, not the gender of the thing being possessed.

Let's study some examples with the words **son** and **sa**.

La femme a son chat *(The woman has her cat).*

Notice that since the word **chat** is masculine, we used the masculine form **son** with it, not the feminine form **sa**, because **son** or **sa** must have the same gender as the thing being possessed.

Also notice that when we translated **son** into English, we translated it with the word *her.* Since the word **son** must agree in gender with the thing being possessed, it doesn't tell us anything about the gender of the person possessing the cat. For that, we must examine the context. When we examine the context of the sentence, we see that the person possessing the cat is female, so we use the word *her* in our English translation. This is different from an English sentence—in an English sentence, *his* or *her* must agree with the gender of the person possessing the item, not the gender of the item itself.

Let's try another example:

L'homme a sa voiture *(The man has his car).*

Again, notice that since the word **voiture** is feminine, we used the feminine **sa** with it, not the masculine form **son**, because **son** or **sa** must have the same gender as the thing being possessed.

When we translated **sa** into English, we translated it with the word *his.* Since the word **sa** must agree in gender with the thing being possessed, it doesn't tell us anything about the gender of the person possessing the car. For that, as before, we must examine the context. When we examine the context of the sentence, we see that the person possessing the car is male, so we use the word *his* in our English translation. As we just mentioned, this is different from an English sentence—in an English sentence, *his* or *her* must agree with the gender of the person possessing the item, not the gender of the item itself.

Here is the point of all this analysis (you might want to memorize this): In an English sentence, *his* or *her* agrees with the gender of the person possessing the thing. In a French sentence, **son** or **sa** agrees with the gender of the noun being possessed.

Also, keep in mind that the plural form of **son** and **sa** is **ses**. **Ses** covers both masculine and feminine, so the gender of the noun being possessed doesn't matter.

Here's something to think about. What if the sentence doesn't provide enough information for you to know the gender of the person who is possessing something? In other words, what if you don't know whether to translate **son**, **sa**, or **ses** as *his* or *her*? Observe this example:

La fille est ma sœur. J'ai son chat. *(The girl is my sister. I have her cat.)*

In this example, the first sentence talks about someone's sister. Therefore, when you get to the second sentence, you know that the word **son** is referring back to the female from the first sentence. She is the cat's owner. This context helps you to know that you should translate **son** as *her*. But what about a sentence like this?

J'ai son chat.

In this example, there isn't enough information for us to know the gender of the person who owns the cat. Therefore, if you were going to translate this sentence into English, you would not know whether to translate **son** as *his* or *her*. If we have an exercise like that in this book, we will put *his/her* in the answer key.

A couple of quick points before we move to the exercises:

- If a feminine noun begins with a vowel, don't use **sa**, use **son**, as in **son amie**. This is the same as what happens with **mon** and **ton**.

- If the word after **son** or **ses** begins with a vowel, there will be a liaison, so you would pronounce the normally silent *n* in **son** or the final *s* in **ses**.

Keeping these grammar rules straight might seem confusing right now, but the key here is practice and repetition. Keep practicing, and these forms will soon become second nature.

EXERCISES:

depends on context.
↓

1. **Ma sœur a son chien.** My sister has his/her dog.
2. **Mon frère a ses chats.** My brother has his/her cats.
3. **Elle a son argent.** She has his/her money.
4. **Monsieur Jones a sa voiture.** Mr. Jones has his/her car.
5. **Elles ont neuf dollars.** They have 9 dollars.
6. **Vous n'avez pas cinq dollars.** Ya'll do not have 5 dollars
7. **J'ai dix euros, mais mon ami n'a pas d'argent.** I have 10 euros, but my friend doesn't have money.
8. **Nous avons un chien, mais nous n'avons pas de chat.** We have a dog, but we don't have a cat
9. **Ils ont de la nourriture.** They have food.
10. **Les enfants ont des livres.** The children have some books

Answers on page 249.

LESSON 78

PLURAL POSSESSIVE ADJECTIVES

Now you know the French way to say *my, your, his,* and *her*. But what if an object belongs to more than one person? In other words, in French, we know how to say *my car*, but how would you say *our car*?

To say *our*, the word is **notre**. And in the plural, it's **nos**. Observe:

> **notre livre** *(our book)*
> **nos livres** *(our books)*

With **notre** and **nos**, there is no separate word for masculine and feminine. It is the same for both genders. The gender of the noun being possessed doesn't matter.

In this book, we have been using the word *y'all* for a second person plural pronoun. In French, the word **votre** means *your*, speaking to more than one person. Therefore in this book, to show that **votre** is addressing more than one person, we will translate it as (gulp) *y'all's*. We know that this probably sounds goofy to some of you, but the point here is to help you differentiate second person singular from second person plural. And remember, the point of this book isn't to teach you English, but to teach you French. Oh, and the plural form of **votre** is **vos**.

> **votre voiture** *(y'all's car)*
> **vos voitures** *(y'all's cars)*

Like **notre** and **nos**, there is no separate word for masculine and feminine with **votre** and **vos**. It is the same for both genders. Again, the gender of the noun being possessed doesn't matter. Furthermore, keep in mind that in the context of formal speech, **votre/vos** can be used to say *your* when speaking to only one person.

To say *their*, the word is **leur**. And in the plural, it's **leurs**.

> **leur chien** *(their dog)*
> **leurs chiens** *(their dogs)*

And, as you might expect, with **leur** and **leurs** there is no separate word for masculine and feminine. And, as with **notre** and **votre**, the gender of the noun being possessed doesn't matter.

For the words **nos**, **vos**, and **leurs**, if the next word starts with a vowel, there will be a liaison, and the normally silent *s* at the end will be pronounced as the first sound of the following word.

Let's put all the possessive adjectives we know into one big chart.

	SINGULAR	PLURAL	
FIRST PERSON	mon/ma/mes	notre/nos	our /ours
SECOND PERSON	ton/ta/tes	votre/vos	your
THIRD PERSON	*his/her* son/sa/ses	leur/leurs	their /theirs

EXERCISES:

1. **Elles ont notre chien !** They have our dog
2. **Il a votre livre.** He has your book
3. **Nous avons leur voiture.** We have their car
4. **Le chien a notre nourriture !** The dog has our food
5. **Nous avons leurs livres.** We have their books
6. **Tu as nos livres.** You have our books
7. **Mon frère a vos chats.** My brother has your cats
8. **Elles ont huit dollars, mais nous n'avons pas d'argent.** They have 8 $ but we do not have money
9. **Monsieur Smith a quatre chats et aussi un chien.** Mr. Smith has 4 cats & also a dog
10. **Il a sa voiture, mais je n'ai pas de voiture.** He has his/her car, but I do not have a car

Answers on page 250.

101

LESSON 79

POSSESSION

Possessive words show ownership of something. In English, we often show possession by using an apostrophe followed by the letter *s*. Observe the following examples:

> <u>Fred's</u> car
> The <u>nation's</u> flag
> <u>Arizona's</u> capital

Sometimes we show possession by using the word *of*.

> The peak <u>of the mountain</u>
> The smell <u>of garlic</u>
> The beginning <u>of the show</u>

Therefore, in English, when you want to show possession of something, you must decide whether to use an apostrophe or the word *of*.

Here are a few of the most basic rules to remember when using apostrophes:

	RULE	EXAMPLE
RULE #1	To make a noun that does not end in *s* possessive, just add an apostrophe and an *s*.	Lauren always wants to borrow Kate's French book.
RULE #2	To make a singular noun that ends in *s* possessive, add an apostrophe and an *s* (just like rule #1).	The class's favorite subject was French.
RULE #3	To make a plural noun that ends in *s* possessive, add an apostrophe to the end of the word.	Due to increased interest in French, all the books' covers are starting to wear out.

LESSON 80

SHOWING POSSESSION IN FRENCH

In the last lesson, we learned that to show possession in English, we can use either an apostrophe and the letter *s* or the word *of*. In English, therefore, there are two ways to show possession.

In French, however, there is only one way, and that is to use the word *of* which in French is **de**. The word **de** is placed directly after the thing that is being possessed, as seen in the following phrase:

le chat de mon père (*my father's cat*)

If you translated it word for word, it would say *the cat of my father*. But a better, smoother translation would be *my father's cat*. Here's another example:

le chien de la femme (*the woman's dog*)

Again, in this example, if you translated it word for word, it would say *the dog of the woman*. But again, it is better and smoother to translate it as *the woman's dog*.

If the next word after **de** starts with a vowel, there will be elision between **de** and the next word. For instance, if your friend André has a cat, you could say this:

le chat d'André (*André's cat*)

EXERCISES:
1. **L'argent de mon frère.** My brother's money
2. **La voiture de la femme.** The woman's car
3. **La nourriture de ma mère.** My mother's food
4. **J'ai le chien de ma sœur.** I have my sister's dog
5. **L'ami de mon frère n'a pas sa voiture.** My brother's friend does not have his car
6. **Le frère d'André a dix euros.** André's friend has 10 euros.
7. **Nous n'avons pas de chien, mais nous avons un chat.** We don't have a dog. but we have a cat.
8. **Tu as notre livre.** You have our book
9. **Vous avez nos livres.** You all have our books
10. **Ils ont vos livres.** They have your books

Answers on page 250.

LESSON 81

MORE ABOUT POSSESSION

There is one more thing we need to tell you about possession: if the word **de** comes before the word **le**, then **de** and **le** will squish together to form the word **du**. So, if you have a sentence like this...

  le chien de le garçon (*the boy's dog*)

...it would be incorrect. Instead, **de** and **le** combine into the word **du**, like this:

  le chien du garçon (*the boy's dog*)

So remember this formula: **de** + **le** = **du**.

In the example above, the word **garçon** was masculine, so it was preceded by the masculine article **le**. But if **de** comes before the feminine article **la**, it doesn't contract into anything.

  le chien de la fille (*the girl's dog*)

Here, **de** and **la** will just stay like they are.

If the word after **le** or **la** starts with a vowel, there will be elision between the article and the noun, and **de** will not contract into anything. Consider these examples:

  le chat de l'ami (*the (male) friend's cat*)
  le chat de l'amie (*the (female) friend's cat*)

These examples are just fine the way they are, and **de** and **l'** won't contract into anything.

EXERCISES:

  1. **La voiture de l'homme.** The man's car.
  2. **Le chat du garçon.** the boy's car

104

3. **L'argent de la fille.** *The girl's money*
4. **J'ai la voiture de mon frère.** *I have my brother's car*
5. **Ton fils a sa voiture.** *Your son has his car*
6. **Ses parents ont sept enfants, mais nous n'avons pas d'enfants.** *His/her parents have 7 children, but we don't have children*
7. **Ils n'ont pas de nourriture.** *They do not have food.*
8. **J'ai du riz, mais tu n'as pas de riz.** *I have rice, but you do not have rice*
9. **Je n'ai pas de livre.** *I do not have a book.*
10. **Elle n'a pas le livre.** *She doesn't have a book*

Answers on page 250.

EXPRESSIONS FRANÇAISES

Sometimes in the news you might hear that a military **coup** has taken place somewhere in the world. The word **coup** is short for the French expression **coup d'état**. That's when the existing government of a country is overthrown.

The word **coup** can mean things like *knockdown, blow,* or *punch.* **D'état** is a combination of **de** and **état**. **De** means **of**, and **état** means *state* or *government*. So **coup d'état** literally means something like *knockdown of government* or *knockdown of state*.

105

LESSON 82

IDIOMS

In conversation, we often use sayings and expressions that carry a meaning other than what the words mean when taken literally. We call these expressions *idioms*.

An idiom could be a saying like this: *I'm still sitting on the fence.* If you say that you are sitting on the fence, it does not mean that you are actually sitting on top of a fence—instead it means that you have not made up your mind about something. So, expressions and sayings like that are called *idioms*.

Other times, we use the term *idiom* to describe phrases in another language that are not translated into English literally. For instance, a phrase commonly found in another language might be worded much differently than that same phrase would be worded in the English language. Therefore, when we translate a French idiom into English, we will not keep the original French wording. Instead, we will translate the meaning of the phrase into English the way an English speaker would normally say it.

LESSON 83

NEW WORDS   **j'ai faim** / **j'ai soif** *"swaf"*

MEANING   *I am hungry / I am thirsty*

PRONUNCIATION TIP: The *m* in **faim** is not fully pronounced. Instead, it gives the vowel sound of **faim** a nasal quality. So, **faim** sounds something like *fah* or *feh*. The *f* in **soif** is not silent. It's one of the "careful" letters, remember?

In English, we say *I am hungry*. But in French, this would be worded a bit differently. This is how you say *I am hungry* in French:

J'ai faim.

J'ai, as you already know, means *I have*. And the word **faim** means *hunger*. So literally, **j'ai faim** means *I have hunger*. But we translate it into English as *I am hungry*.

If you want to say *I am thirsty*, the situation is exactly the same:

J'ai soif.

The word **soif** means *thirst*. So literally, **j'ai soif** means *I have thirst*. But we translate it into English as *I am thirsty*.

If someone else is hungry or thirsty, just use the different forms of **j'ai** along with **faim** or **soif**, as shown in these examples:

Il a faim (*He is hungry*).
Nous avons soif (*We are thirsty*).

If someone is not hungry, just negate the verb **j'ai**, like this:

Mon chat n'a pas faim (*My cat is not hungry*).
Les enfants n'ont pas faim (*The children are not hungry*).

107

The following exercises will give you some practice using these expressions.

EXERCISES:

1. **J'ai faim.** _I am hungry_
2. **Je n'ai pas faim.** _I am not hungry_
3. **Le chien du garçon n'a pas soif.** _The boy's dog is not thirsty_
4. **Nos chats ont soif.** _Our cats are thirsty_
5. **Tu n'as pas leur voiture.** _You do not have their car_
6. **Ma fille a la voiture de mon frère.** _My sister has my brother's car_
7. **Mon chien a faim, mais il n'a pas de nourriture.** _My dog is hungry but he does not have food_
8. **Vous avez nos livres.** _You all have our books_
9. **Nous avons de la nourriture, mais vous n'avez pas faim.** _we have some food, but You'll are not hungry_
10. **Tu as notre chien et aussi son chien.**
   You have our dog and also his dog

Answers on page 251.

LESSON 84

NEW WORD   **je veux**

MEANING   *I want*

When we learned about **j'ai**, we learned each form one at a time. But now that you have some experience working with verbs, there is no need to learn every new verb one form at a time. So, in this lesson, we are going to give you all the forms of **je veux** at the same time.

Take some time to memorize these forms along with their accompanying pronouns.

vouloir

	SINGULAR	PLURAL
FIRST PERSON	**je veux**	**nous voulons**
SECOND PERSON	**tu veux**	**vous voulez**
THIRD PERSON	**il/elle veut**	**ils/elles veulent**

In lesson 76, we talked at length about sentences that say *I don't have any....* We showed you that if the noun you don't have is singular, plural, countable, uncountable, masculine, or feminine, use the word **de** before it to say that you don't have it. But if it has a definite article in front of it, don't use **de** and let the noun keep its definite article.

This same concept will apply to not only the verb **j'ai**, but to other action verbs, too, such as **je veux**, the new verb for this lesson. Compare these two sentences:

Je veux un chien (*I want a dog*).
Je ne veux pas de chien (*I do not want a dog*).

Notice that **un** changed to **de** in the second sentence, which was negative.

109

But as we mentioned before, this rule does not apply to nouns with a definite article. If you are using a definite article to refer to a specific thing, go ahead and keep the definite article if the sentence is negated. Compare these two sentences:

> **Je veux le chien** (*I want the dog*).
> **Je ne veux pas le chien** (*I do not want the dog*).

Notice that in the second sentence, we kept the definite article **le** even though the verb was negated.

EXERCISES:

1. **Je veux de l'argent.** I want money
2. **Tu veux la voiture de l'homme, mais je ne veux pas la voiture.** You want the man of the car, but I do not want the car
3. **Il veut dix dollars, mais nous n'avons pas d'argent.** He wants 10 $ but we do not have money
4. **Nous ne voulons pas de chat.** we do not want any cat
5. **Mon chien a faim, mais il n'a pas de nourriture.** My dog is hongrey, but he does not have food
6. **Mon frère n'a pas de chien, mais son fils veut un chien.** My brother does not have a dog, but his son wants a dog.
7. **J'ai soif, mais vous n'avez pas soif.** I am thirsty but you are not thirsty
8. **Nos enfants veulent notre argent et aussi notre voiture.** our children want our money, but also want our car
9. **Ma sœur a nos chiens et nous avons ses chiens.** My sister has our dogs and we have her dogs
10. **Il a vos chiens et aussi leurs chiens.** He has your dogs and also their dogs.

Answers on page 251.

LESSON 85

NEW WORDS **parce que**

MEANING *because*

PRONUNCIATION TIP: **Parce que** sounds something like *pahrs-kuh.*

If the word after **parce que** starts with a vowel, there will be elision. For instance, if the word after **parce que** is **elle**, it would look like this:

parce qu'elle

EXERCISES:

1. **Tu veux de la nourriture parce que tu as faim.** *You want food b/c you are hungry*
2. **Il n'a pas de voiture parce qu'il n'a pas d'argent.** *He has no car b/c he has no money*
3. **Nous avons faim, mais ils n'ont pas de nourriture.** *We are hungry but they do not have food*
4. **Mon mari veut une fille et un fils aussi.** *My husband wants a girl & a boy*
5. **Les enfants veulent sept dollars.** *The children want 7 dollars.*
6. **Vous avez un chien, mais vous voulez un chat.** *Y'all have a dog, but y'all want a cat.*
7. **Je veux la voiture de mon père parce que je n'ai pas de voiture.** *I want the car of my father b/c I do not have a car*
8. **Elle veut de la nourriture parce qu'elle a faim.** *She wants food b/c she is hungry*
9. **Leurs chats ont soif parce qu'ils n'ont pas d'eau.** *Their cats are thirsty b/c they have no water*
10. **Votre chien a notre dinde !** *Your dog has our turkey.*

Answers on page 251.

LESSON 86

NEW WORD   **eau**

MEANING   *water*

PRONUNCIATION TIP: **Eau** sounds like *oh.*

Eau is a feminine noun.

If you wanted to say *some water,* you would use a partitive article in the same way you would with other foods, like this:

Je veux de l'eau *(I want some water).*

EXERCISES:

1. **Je veux de l'eau parce que j'ai soif.** I want water b/c I am thirsty
2. **Ils veulent de l'eau parce qu'ils ont soif.** They want water b/c they are thirsty
3. **Mon père a faim et il veut de la nourriture.** My father is hungry and he wants food
4. **Nous avons faim, mais nous n'avons pas d'argent.** We are hungry but we do not have money
5. **Elle veut la voiture de son père.** She wants the car of her father
6. **Vous voulez nos chats.** You all want our cats
7. **Tu veux de la dinde parce que tu as faim.** You want turkey b/c you are hungry
8. **Je veux leur voiture.** I want their car.
9. **Mon frère a son argent—douze euros, huit dollars et aussi trois francs.** my brother has his/her money - 12 euros, 8 dollars, y also 3 francs
10. **J'ai onze chats, mais je n'ai pas d'amis.** I have 11 cats, but I don't have friends

Answers on page 252.

LESSON 87

NEW WORD   **je parle**

MEANING   *I speak*

Je parle is our first *regular verb*. A regular verb is a verb that follows a predictable pattern. Observe the following chart:

	SINGULAR	PLURAL
FIRST PERSON	**je parle**	**nous parlons**
SECOND PERSON	**tu parles**	**vous parlez**
THIRD PERSON	**il/elle parle**	**ils/elles parlent**

In order to translate the exercises for this lesson, there are two important words you will need to know: **anglais** and **français**. The word **anglais** is the French word for *English* and **français** is the French word for… well, you guessed it—*French*. Notice that the French words **anglais** and **français** are not capitalized as they would be in English. Also, you do not need an article in front of **anglais** or **français**. In other words, you would say **je parle francais**, not **je parle le français**.

EXERCISES:

1. **Je parle anglais.** I speak english
2. **Vous parlez français.** You speak french
3. **Mes parents parlent anglais.** My parents speak english
4. **Nous parlons français et aussi anglais.** We speak french but also english
5. **Nous voulons du riz, mais ils veulent de la dinde.** We want rice but they want turkey
6. **Il ne parle pas français.** He does not speak french
7. **Nous avons soif parce que nous n'avons pas d'eau.** "duell we are thirsty b/c we do not have water.
8. **Le chat de la femme a faim—il veut de la nourriture.** The woman's cat is hungry, he wants food.
9. **Les enfants ont faim et soif—ils veulent de l'eau.** The children are hungry and thirsty — they want water
10. **Ils veulent notre nourriture parce qu'ils n'ont pas leur nourriture.** They want our food because they do not have food

Answers on page 252.

LESSON 88

THE PRESENT TENSE

In this book, all the verbs that we will learn about are present tense verbs. This means that the action happening is in the here and now. But did you know that there is more than one kind of present tense?

In English, you might see a sentence like this:

> I speak French.

Even though you may not be speaking French right this minute, it is still a current fact—therefore, we use the present tense to express it. This kind of present tense is called the *simple present*.

Contrast that with this similar English sentence:

> I am speaking French.

In this sentence, the verb *speaking* communicates a different shade of meaning than in the first example. Here, you are saying that at this very moment you are speaking the French language—the action is happening right now! This kind of present tense is called the *present progressive*. It's progressive because the action is ongoing at this very moment.

So how does this relate to French verbs? What we want you to understand is that in English, there is both a simple present and a present progressive, but in French there is not. In French, there is only one way to say something in the present tense. Observe this French sentence:

Je parle français.

If you translate this sentence into English, you could translate it as either *I speak French* or *I am speaking French*.

How will you know whether to translate a verb using simple present or present progressive? Look at the context, and that should make it clear. For example, if you saw a French sentence that contains the verb **je parle** and you aren't sure what the best translation is, try translating it as both *I speak* and *I am speaking* and see which one sounds better.

EXPRESSIONS FRANÇAISES

To say that something is the best of the best, you say that it is the **crème de la crème**. The word **crème** (pronounced *krem*) means *cream*. Therefore, **crème de la crème** literally means *cream of the cream*. A similar saying in English would be *the cream of the crop*.

You might say that this book is the **crème de la crème** of French books.

LESSON 89

NEW WORDS **tous les jours**

MEANING *every day*

Now let's learn how to say *every day* in French:

tous les jours

Tous is the plural form of the adjective **tout** which means *all*. The word **jours** is the plural form of the word **jour** which means *day*. Since **jours** is masculine and plural, it needs to have **les** as its article.

If you translated **tous les jours** word for word, it would say *all the days*. But we translate it into English as *every day*.

EXERCISES:

1. **Je parle anglais tous les jours.** I speak english every day.
2. **Mon chat veut notre nourriture tous les jours.** Our cat wants our food every day.
3. **Tous les jours, tu parles français.** Every day, you speak french
4. **Elle a un chat et quatre chiens, et ses chiens ont faim.** She has a cat and 4 dogs, and her dogs are hungry.
5. **Nous avons douze euros, mais nous n'avons pas de francs.** We have 12 euros, but we do not have francs
6. **Votre sœur est mon amie.** Your sister is my friend
7. **Elles parlent français tous les jours, mais nous parlons anglais.** They speak french every day, but we speak english
8. **Mon chien veut de la nourriture tous les jours.** My dog wants food every day.
9. **Nous voulons de l'eau parce que nous avons soif.** We want water b/c we are thirsty.
10. **Les amis de mon papa ont faim, mais nous n'avons pas de nourriture.**
    The friends of my dad are hungry, but we do not have food.

Answers on page 252.

116

LESSON 90

STEMS AND PERSONAL ENDINGS

You may have noticed by now that there is a pattern to the endings of French verbs. For instance, first person plural verbs typically end in *-ons*, as seen in words like **avons** and **voulons**.

Let's take a closer look at the verb **je parle** for a moment. For convenience, here are all the forms of **je parle** again:

	SINGULAR	PLURAL
FIRST PERSON	je parle	nous parlons
SECOND PERSON	tu parles	vous parlez
THIRD PERSON	il/elle parle	ils/elles parlent

 *said the same*

Notice that each form of **je parle** starts with *parl–*. That part of the verb is called the *stem*. After the stem, each different form of the verb has its own special, individual ending. If we isolated those endings and put them into a chart, the chart would look like this:

	SINGULAR	PLURAL
FIRST PERSON	-e	-ons
SECOND PERSON	-es	-ez
THIRD PERSON	-e	-ent

We will call these endings *personal endings*. They show whether a verb is first person, second person, or third person, and also whether the verb is singular or plural.

When you understand how verb stems and personal endings work, it's much easier to understand and use French verbs. There are certain rules to follow and patterns to learn, too. From here to the end of the book, we will mention these patterns and rules in the book a little, but we will discuss them more in the commentary recordings.

As we finish up this lesson, here's an important point to remember: the personal endings we showed you in the chart above only work for *regular verbs*. Irregular verbs are a different story!

LESSON 91

WHY DOES FRENCH HAVE PERSONAL ENDINGS?

In the last lesson, we learned that French verbs have special endings called *personal endings*. These personal endings indicate whether a verb is first person, second person, or third person, and also whether the verb is singular or plural. But why do French verbs have these personal endings in the first place?

Well, to make a long story short, the French language is a direct descendant of Latin, the language of the ancient Romans. Whenever the Romans conquered and occupied a territory, they brought their language, Latin, with them. For a long time, Latin was spoken throughout a large part of Europe. But later, after the fall of the Roman Empire, the Latin that was spoken in places like France, Spain, and Italy gradually changed into French, Spanish, and Italian. That's why many French words are so closely related to Latin words. The French verb system is derived from Latin, and so is much of the vocabulary.

Here's an example of what I mean: the Latin word **sumus** means *we are*. Over time, the way this word was pronounced gradually changed. People started to pronounce the vowels differently, and they stopped pronouncing the *s* at the end, leaving the French word **sommes**.

Here's another example: the Latin word **filius** means *son*. Over time, people started to pronounce this word in a more compacted way, leaving out the *l* sound in the middle. The gradual pronunciation changes resulted in the word **fils**.

On the next page there is a box with some Latin words on the left and their French derivatives on the right. Just for fun, see if you can match each Latin word with its French derivative.

mundus *(world)*	temps
pānis *(bread)*	paix
saeculum *(age, century)*	siècle
amīcus *(friend)*	mort
liber *(book)*	cœur
ecclēsia *(church)*	pain
tempus *(time)*	livre
cor *(heart)*	corps
corpus *(body)*	église
pax *(peace)*	monde
mors, mortis *(death)*	ami

Answers on page 253.

LESSON 92

NEW WORD   **j'achète**

MEANING   *I buy*

Take a look at the chart below, and examine the different forms of our new verb for this lesson. Look especially at the accent marks. What did you notice?

In the singular forms of this verb, there is an accent mark on the second syllable. There is also an accent mark on the second syllable of the third person plural form. All four of these accented forms will sound something like *ah-SHET*. But in the first person plural and second person plural forms, the *e* is there, but it may or may not be pronounced depending on how fast the speaker is speaking. For example, if someone is speaking quickly, the first person plural form, **achetons**, sounds something like *ash-toh*.

Use this handy chart to memorize the forms of **j'achète**.

	SINGULAR	PLURAL
FIRST PERSON	j'achète	*we* nous achetons
SECOND PERSON	tu achètes	vous achetez
THIRD PERSON	il/elle achète	ils/elles achètent

EXERCISES:

1. **Tous les jours j'achète de la nourriture.** everyday I buy food
2. **Nous achetons de la nourriture tous les jours.** We buy food everyday
3. **Les hommes n'achètent pas de nourriture tous les jours.** The men do not buy food everyday
4. **Le chat de ma sœur a faim, mais ma sœur n'a pas de nourriture.** The cat of my sister is hungry, but my sister does not have food
5. **Je n'ai pas de nourriture et je n'ai pas d'argent.** I do not have food, and I do not have money
6. **Tu parles anglais, mais je parle français.** You speak english but I speak french

121

My father does not has his car - he has the car of his brother

7. **Mon père n'a pas sa voiture—il a la voiture de son frère.**

8. **Ma sœur ne parle pas anglais, mais elle parle français.**

My sister does not speak english but she speaks french

9. **Nous parlons français tous les jours, mais ils ne parlent pas anglais.**

We speak french all day but they do not speak english

10. **Je n'achète pas la voiture !**

I did not buy the car.

Answers on page 253.

LESSON 93

ASKING QUESTIONS IN FRENCH

Questions are an important part of any conversation. Fortunately for us, it is very easy to ask questions in French. Imagine you have the following sentence:

Tu parles anglais. *(You speak English.)*

To turn this into a question, all you have to do is add in the phrase **est-ce que**, which sounds something like *ess-kuh.*

Est-ce que tu parles anglais ? *(Do you speak English?)*

DO

Est-ce que literally means *is it that?* Therefore, the statement **Est-ce que tu parles anglais ?** would literally say *Is it that you speak English?* But a smoother, better-sounding translation would be *Do you speak English?*

Using **est-ce que** to ask a question is only one out of four possible methods of asking questions in French. In this book, we will focus only on this particular method because it is easy to learn and it is commonly used in both formal and informal situations.

One final note: if the word after **est-ce que** begins with a vowel, there will be elision, like this:

Est-ce qu'elle a un chat ? *(Does she have a cat?)*

DO we

1. **Est-ce que nous avons notre voiture ?** Do we have our car?
2. **Est-ce qu'ils achètent de la nourriture tous les jours ?** Do they buy food everyday?
3. **Est-ce que tu as un chat ?** Do you have a cat?
4. **Est-ce que vous avez trois chiens ?** Do y'all have 3 dogs?
5. **Est-ce que tu veux la voiture de ton père ?** Do you want the car of your father?
6. **Est-ce qu'elle est ton amie ?** Is she your friend.
7. **Est-ce que nous avons du riz ?** Do we have rice?
8. **Est-ce que le chat a votre nourriture ?** Does the cat have your food.
9. **Son chien a de la nourriture, mais il n'a pas faim.** his/her dog has food, but he is not hungry.
10. **Le frère de mon père a faim parce qu'il n'a pas de nourriture.** The brother of my father is hungry is b/c he does not have food

Answers on page 253.

123

LESSON 94

NEW WORDS   **oui / non**

MEANING   *yes / no*

PRONUNCIATION TIP: **Oui** sounds somewhat similar to the English word *we*. The *n* in **non** is silent, so it sounds something like *noh*, with a nasal sound.

Now that you know how to ask questions, you need to know how to answer them— so read the following instructions very carefully:

Oui means *yes*. **Non** means *no*.

We know this is a difficult lesson, but try not to get discouraged.

EXERCISES:

1. **Est-ce que tu achètes de la nourriture tous les jours ?** *Do you buy food every day?*
2. **Non, je n'achète pas de nourriture tous les jours.** *No, I do not buy food every day.*
3. **Est-ce que votre frère a un enfant ?** *Does your brother have a child*
4. **Oui, notre frère a trois fils. Il a aussi une fille.** *Yes, our brother has 3 sons. He also has a daughter*
5. **Est-ce que les hommes ont faim ?** *Are the men hungry?*
6. **Oui, les hommes ont faim, mais nous n'avons pas de nourriture.** *Yes, the men are hungry but they do not have food*
7. **Est-ce que tu es une mère ?** *Are you a mother?*
8. **Non, je ne suis pas une mère parce que je n'ai pas d'enfants.** *No, I am not a mother b/c I do not have children*
9. **Est-ce que tu parles français ?** *Do you speak French?*
10. **Non, je parle anglais, mais mes sœurs parlent français tous les jours.** *No, I speak english but my sisters speak french every day.*

Answers on page 254.

124

LESSON 95

MANGER

NEW WORD   **je mange**

MEANING   *I eat*

Learn the forms of **je mange** with this handy chart:

	SINGULAR	PLURAL
FIRST PERSON	**je mange**	**nous mangeons** *joh*
SECOND PERSON	**tu manges**	**vous mangez**
THIRD PERSON	**il/elle mange**	**ils/elles mangent**

There is something you should notice about this verb. Think for a moment about what you have learned about verb stems and personal endings. Then, carefully examine the six verb forms above. Do you notice anything strange?

The first person plural form, **mangeons**, has the letter *e* wedged between the stem and the personal ending. Why? The answer has to do with pronunciation. You see, in French, before the letter *o*, the letter *g* has a hard *g* sound like the *g* in *go*. But in the word **mangeons**, the letter *g* is supposed to have a soft *g* sound. Therefore, the letter *e* in **mangeons** is telling us to pronounce the *g* like the *s* in the word *vision*.

EXERCISES:

1. **Je mange de la nourriture tous les jours.** *I eat food everyday*
2. **Les garçons mangent de la nourriture tous les jours.** *The boys eat food everyday*
3. **Nous mangeons tous les jours.** *We eat everyday.*
4. **Est-ce que madame Jones a faim ?** *Is mrs. Jones hungry?.*
5. **Non, madame Jones n'a pas faim, mais j'ai faim.** *No, mrs. Jones is not hungry but I*
6. **Ils achètent de la nourriture tous les jours.** *They buy food everyday am hungry*
7. **Les enfants de ma sœur veulent de l'eau parce qu'ils ont soif.**
   The children of my sister want water b/c they are thirsty

125

8. **Le chat mange notre dinde !** The cat eats our turkey.
9. **Nous parlons français, mais vous ne parlez pas français.** We speak French but do not speak French
10. **Elle n'achète pas de voiture parce que son mari n'a pas d'argent.**
    She does not buy a car b/c her husband doesn't have money.

Answers on page 254.

EXPRESSIONS FRANÇAISES

Have you ever been offered an **hors d'œuvre** at a party?

The word **hors** means *out* or *outside*. **De** means *of*. The word **œuvre** means *work* as in something you make or build. So, the expression **hors d'œuvre** means *outside of the work*. An **hors d'œuvre** is a small appetizer served to guests before the meal—in other words, it's outside of or apart from the main meal.

Hors d'œuvre is pronounced something like *or-duhvr*.

126

LESSON 96

NEW WORD   **toujours**

MEANING   *always*

The word **toujours** comes from two French words: **tous**, which means *all*, and **jours**, which means *days*. So literally **toujours** means *all days*, but we translate it into English as *always*.

As you may have noticed, **tous les jours** and **toujours** come from the same words, so don't confuse them.

Toujours is an adverb. In a sentence, it goes immediately after the verb.

EXERCISES:

1. **Nous parlons toujours français.**
2. **Ils mangent toujours de la dinde.**
3. **Tu achètes de la nourriture tous les jours.**
4. **Est-ce que ton frère a la voiture ?**
5. **Oui, mon frère a la voiture.**
6. **Non, mon frère n'a pas la voiture.**
7. **Je mange du riz tous les jours.**
8. **Le chat de ma fille veut de l'eau parce qu'il a soif.**
9. **Vos fils n'ont pas leurs livres.**
10. **Vos enfants ont faim et ils ont soif aussi.**

Answers on page 254.

LESSON 97

NEW WORD   **je bois**

MEANING   *I drink*

This verb doesn't follow any predictable pattern. All its forms must be memorized.

	SINGULAR	PLURAL
FIRST PERSON	**je bois**	**nous buvons**
SECOND PERSON	**tu bois**	**vous buvez**
THIRD PERSON	**il/elle boit**	**ils/elles boivent**

EXERCISES:

1. **Je bois toujours de l'eau.**
2. **Elle a soif, mais elle ne veut pas d'eau.**
3. **Leurs frères parlent français tous les jours.**
4. **Est-ce que tu bois de l'eau tous les jours ?**
5. **Oui, nous buvons de l'eau tous les jours.**
6. **Elle mange de la nourriture parce qu'elle a faim.**
7. **Mes parents achètent de la nourriture tous les jours.**
8. **Mes chiens mangent de la nourriture et boivent de l'eau tous les jours.**
9. **Mon papa a quatre chiens, mais il n'a pas de chat.**
10. **Elle veut l'argent de son père parce qu'elle veut une voiture.**

Answers on page 255.

LESSON 98

NEW WORDS **toutes les semaines**

MEANING *every week*

You already know how to say *every day*. Now we are going to learn how to say *every week*. This is how it's done:

toutes les semaines

Semaine is a feminine noun that means *week*. Since **semaines** is feminine and plural, it needs the article **les** and the adjective **toutes**, which means *all*.

If you translated **toutes les semaines** word for word, it would say *all the weeks*. But we translate it into English as *every week*.

EXERCISES:

1. **Vous achetez de la nourriture toutes les semaines.**
2. **Notre mère achète de la nourriture toutes les semaines.**
3. **Tes parents achètent de la nourriture toutes les semaines.**
4. **Le chien de ma mère a faim parce qu'il n'a pas de nourriture.**
5. **Nous voulons de la nourriture et de l'argent.**
6. **Mes chats veulent toujours ma nourriture.**
7. **La fille d'André parle anglais et aussi français.**
8. **Les hommes sont mes frères et les femmes sont mes sœurs.**
9. **Est-ce que vous voulez une voiture ?**
10. **Non, je ne veux pas de voiture.**

Answers on page 255.

LESSON 99

MEANING   *I work*

PRONUNCIATION TIP: The end of the word **travaille** sounds somewhat like the English word *eye*. Therefore **travaille** sounds something like *trav-eye*. You may even hear a final *yuh* sound if the speaker is speaking slowly.

Je travaille is a regular verb. This means that the endings follow the expected pattern (unlike an irregular verb).

	SINGULAR	PLURAL
FIRST PERSON	**je travaille**	**nous travaillons**
SECOND PERSON	**tu travailles**	**vous travaillez**
THIRD PERSON	**il/elle travaille**	**ils/elles travaillent**

EXERCISES:

1. **Je travaille tous les jours.**
2. **Nos sœurs travaillent tous les jours.**
3. **Nous achetons de la nourriture toutes les semaines.**
4. **Est-ce que l'amie de ton frère travaille tous les jours ?**
5. **Oui, elle travaille tous les jours.**
6. **Nous buvons de l'eau tous les jours.**
7. **Ils ne parlent pas anglais, mais ils parlent français.**
8. **Nous avons soif parce que nous n'avons pas d'eau.**
9. **Mes amis ont toujours de l'argent parce qu'ils travaillent tous les jours.**
10. **Mon chien boit son eau et il veut aussi sa nourriture.**

Answers on page 255.

LESSON 100

GOING PLACES

In French, to say that you are going somewhere, you need the verb **je vais. Je vais** means *I go* or *I am going*. Observe the different forms of **je vais** in this handy chart.

	SINGULAR	PLURAL
FIRST PERSON	**je vais**	**nous allons**
SECOND PERSON	**tu vas**	**vous allez**
THIRD PERSON	**il/elle va**	**ils/elles vont**

Notice that this verb is irregular. The first person plural and second person plural forms (**allons** and **allez**) are the only regular forms of this verb. The other forms start out with a completely different spelling.

Take some time to memorize these verb forms, and over the next couple of lessons we will start putting together some sentences with **je vais.**

LESSON 101

PREPOSITIONS

A *preposition* is a word that shows a relationship or connection between two nouns. Examples of prepositions are *in, below, above,* and *beside.* Here's an example of a sentence with a preposition.

The bicycle is inside the garage.

In that sentence, the word *inside* was the preposition. Notice that in this sentence there are two items being talked about: the bicycle and the garage. The preposition showed the relationship between the two items.

The person saying this sentence wants to tell someone about the location of the bicycle. There are several ways to tell someone the location of an item. The speaker could have indicated the location of the bicycle a different way—if the speaker happened to be near the bicycle, he or she could have pointed at it and said, "It's over here," or "It's over there." But with a preposition, you don't have to be near the object you want to talk about—you can show its location by using something else as a point of reference.

Let's look at that sentence again and observe how the speaker used the garage as a way to specify the location of the bicycle.

The bicycle is inside the garage.

The speaker used the garage as a point of reference to show where the bicycle was. The preposition *inside* referred directly to the garage. In grammatical terms, the word that the preposition refers to is called the *object of the preposition.*

Therefore, in this sentence, the word *inside* is the preposition and the word *garage* is the object of the preposition.

Just for practice, in each of the following sentences, see if you can spot the preposition and the object of the preposition.

EXERCISES:

1. Your book fell behind the couch.
2. Just put that plant beside the lamp.
3. The spare tire is in the trunk.
4. We drove through the tunnel.
5. I just saw a chipmunk run under the house!
6. I want to get this done before lunch.
7. After school, the accordion ensemble will rehearse again.
8. The new store is by the post office.
9. You aren't allowed to do that on campus.
10. Have you ever wondered what is beyond that mountain?

Answers on page 256.

LESSON 102

NEW WORD   **à**

MEANING   *to*

Our new word for this lesson, **à**, is a preposition. Notice that it has an accent mark over it, so don't confuse it with the verb **a**, which we studied earlier.

The word **à** is a very useful word that will really have you going places! But right now, we don't have any places to go, so let's learn a couple of new words. Most people go to the store and the bank on a regular basis, so let's learn how to say *store* (as in grocery store) and *bank* in French.

The most common word for *store* in French is **magasin**. The French word for *bank* is **banque**. That one shouldn't be too hard to remember! By the way, **magasin** is masculine and **banque** is feminine.

Now that we have some places to go, let's use the word **à** in a couple of short examples:

    à la banque *(to the bank)*

In that example, we saw the preposition **à** followed by the article **la** since the word **banque** is feminine. However, when **à** is followed by a masculine noun, something special happens, as seen in this example:

    à le magasin *(to the store)*

In a sentence like that, when **à** is followed by the article **le**, **à** and **le** squish together into the word **au**, like this:

    au magasin *(to the store)*

So while you translate the exercises for this lesson, remember that **à + le = au. Au** is pronounced *oh.*

134

EXERCISES:

1. Ma mère va à la banque toutes les semaines.
2. Nous allons au magasin toutes les semaines.
3. Est-ce que tes parents vont au magasin tous les jours ?
4. Non, ils vont au magasin toutes les semaines.
5. Je vais à la banque parce que je n'ai pas d'argent.
6. Les garçons et les filles travaillent tous les jours.
7. Tu bois de l'eau tous les jours parce que tu as toujours soif.
8. Je veux la voiture d'André, mais je n'ai pas d'argent.
9. Nous n'achetons pas de voiture parce que nous n'avons pas d'argent.
10. L'amie de ma mère parle anglais. Elle parle aussi français.

Answers on page 256.

LESSON 103

NEW WORDS   **centre commercial**

MEANING   *mall, shopping center*

Centre commercial is a masculine noun. It can mean *mall* or *shopping center*, but in this book we will just use it to mean *mall*.

EXERCISES:

1. **Nous allons au centre commercial toutes les semaines.**
2. **Mes amis vont au centre commercial tous les jours.**
3. **Ma fille va au centre commercial toutes les semaines.**
4. **Est-ce que tu vas à la banque toutes les semaines ?**
5. **Oui, je vais à la banque toutes les semaines.**
6. **Mes enfants veulent un chat.**
7. **Nous allons au centre commercial toutes les semaines parce que nous sommes amis.**
8. **Nous ne mangeons pas de riz parce que nous n'avons pas de riz.**
9. **Leurs enfants travaillent toujours, mais nos enfants ne travaillent pas.**
10. **Ma sœur a un chat, et son chat veut de l'eau parce qu'il a soif.**

Answers on page 257.

LESSON 104

MORE ABOUT À

A couple of lessons ago, we learned that the preposition **à** means *to*. But in addition to showing where you are going, the word **à** can also mean *at*. As you observe the following example sentence, remember that **à + le = au**:

    Je suis au magasin *(I am at the store)*.

The context of the sentence will make it clear whether **à** means *to* or *at*.

EXERCISES:

1. **Je vais au magasin.**
2. **Je suis au magasin.**
3. **Mon père va à la banque.**
4. **Ma mère travaille à la banque tous les jours.**
5. **Notre père est au magasin.**
6. **Des amis vont au centre commercial.**
7. **Est-ce que vous buvez de l'eau tous les jours ?**
8. **Oui, je bois de l'eau tous les jours parce que j'ai toujours soif.**
9. **Mon frère et ses enfants vont au centre commercial.**
10. **Mon chat mange sa nourriture.**

Answers on page 257.

LESSON 105

NEW WORD   **parc**

MEANING   *park*

Parc, our new word for this lesson, is masculine.

EXERCISES:

1. **Je suis au parc.**
2. **Elles vont au magasin toutes les semaines.**
3. **Est-ce que tu vas au parc tous les jours ?**
4. **Non, mais je vais au parc toutes les semaines.**
5. **Nous parlons toujours français, mais mes parents ne parlent pas français.**
6. **Nous n'allons pas au centre commercial parce que nos parents n'ont pas d'argent.**
7. **L'amie de ma sœur travaille à la banque.**
8. **Il boit toujours de l'eau.**
9. **Je veux une voiture, mais nous n'achetons pas de voiture.**
10. **Nous mangeons au centre commercial toutes les semaines.**

Answers on page 257.

LESSON 106

NEW WORD   **avec**

MEANING   *with*

PRONUNCIATION TIP: The *c* at the end of **avec** is not silent, so **avec** sounds something like *ah-veck*. **Avec** follows the "careful" rule.

Avec is another preposition, just like **à**.

EXERCISES:

1. **Je vais au parc avec mes amis.**
2. **Je mange avec mes sœurs au centre commercial toutes les semaines.**
3. **Il travaille avec mon frère tous les jours au magasin de mon père.**
4. **Je parle anglais avec mes amis, mais je parle toujours français avec mes parents.**
5. **Je bois de l'eau tous les jours.**
6. **Vous parlez français tous les jours.**
7. **Mes enfants ne parlent pas anglais, mais ils parlent français.**
8. **Est-ce que nous avons de la nourriture ?**
9. **Nous n'avons pas d'argent, mais l'ami de mon père a deux dollars.**
10. **Ma mère va à la banque parce qu'elle veut de l'argent.**

Answers on page 258.

LESSON 107

STRESSED PRONOUNS

In the last lesson you learned about the preposition **avec**. We used it to say things like *with my brother* or *with my friends*.

But what if you wanted to say something like *with me* or *with you*? Words such as *me* and *you* are pronouns. We already know how to say pronouns in French, right? Here are the pronouns we know so far.

	SINGULAR	PLURAL
FIRST PERSON	**je**	**nous**
SECOND PERSON	**tu**	**vous**
THIRD PERSON	**il/elle**	**ils/elles**

These pronouns have taken us a long way—but unfortunately, we can't use these particular pronouns for every purpose. A pronoun can play different roles within a sentence. For example, when a pronoun is the subject of a sentence, it is playing a different role than if it is the object of a preposition. In French, we need one kind of pronoun to be the subject of a sentence and a different kind of pronoun to be the object of a preposition.

Here is how this works out in French. When the speaker is the subject of a sentence, he or she uses the word **je** to mean *I*. But if the speaker is the object of a preposition, the speaker cannot use **je**. In other words, you can't say this:

avec je *(with I)*

That would be wrong—like saying *with I* in English. Instead, you must use a special kind of pronoun called a *stressed pronoun*. Stressed pronouns are the pronouns you use when the pronoun is the object of a preposition. In this case, the stressed pronoun would be **moi**, so that would give you this:

avec moi (*with me*)

Likewise, when you want the word *he* to be the subject of the sentence, you can use the French word **il** to mean *he*. But if you want that same word to be the object of a preposition, you can't use the word **il**. In other words, you can't say this:

avec il (*with he*)

That would be wrong—like saying *with he* in English. Again, we need a stressed pronoun here because it's the object of the preposition. In this case, the stressed pronoun would be **lui**, so that would give you this:

avec lui (*with him*)

By now, you get the idea about what stressed pronouns are and how they are used. Here is a complete chart of stressed pronouns in French:

	SINGULAR	PLURAL
FIRST PERSON	**moi**	**nous**
SECOND PERSON	**toi**	**vous**
THIRD PERSON	**lui** / **elle**	**eux** / **elles**

As you can see, some stressed pronouns are identical to the subject pronouns, but four of them are different. We have circled these for your convenience. Use the chart provided to become familiar with stressed pronouns, then use the following exercises to get some practice working with them.

EXERCISES:

1. **Les filles vont au centre commercial avec moi toutes les semaines.**
2. **Est-ce qu'il mange avec toi toutes les semaines ?**
3. **Je vais au parc avec eux tous les jours.**
4. **Nous allons au parc avec lui toutes les semaines.**
5. **Les filles veulent de l'eau parce qu'elles ont soif.**
6. **Ton chien veut de l'eau, mais notre chien n'a pas soif.**

7. **Mon frère travaille avec moi tous les jours.**
8. **L'ami de ma mère parle français, mais je parle anglais.**
9. **Monsieur Smith travaille au magasin tous les jours avec ses enfants.**
10. **Nos chiens boivent toujours de l'eau.**

Answers on page 258.

EXPRESSIONS FRANÇAISES

If you want to disagree with someone, you can start out your side of the story with the French expression **au contraire**.

Au typically translates as *to the* or *at the*. **Contraire** means *opposite*. So, literally **au contraire** says *to the opposite*. A similar English saying would be *on the contrary*.

LESSON 108

NEW WORD   **plage**

MEANING   *beach*

PRONUNCIATION TIP: The *g* in **plage** is pronounced like the *s* in *vision*. So, **plage** has only one syllable, and rhymes (sort of) with the *Taj* in Taj Mahal.

Plage, our new word for this lesson, is feminine.

EXERCISES:

1. **Est-ce que tu vas à la plage ?**
2. **Mes amis vont à la plage avec moi toutes les semaines.**
3. **Nous sommes à la plage avec notre chien.**
4. **Il va à la plage avec ses parents toutes les semaines.**
5. **Ils vont toujours à la plage, mais nous allons toujours au parc.**
6. **Elle va à la plage avec lui toutes les semaines.**
7. **Elles sont à la plage avec leurs amies.**
8. **Je veux la voiture de ma sœur parce que je n'ai pas de voiture.**
9. **Il ne va pas au magasin avec toi.**
10. **J'achète de la nourriture tous les jours au magasin.**

Answers on page 258.

LESSON 109

NEW WORD **souvent**

MEANING *often*

This is your second French adverb. It comes immediately after the verb just like **toujours**.

EXERCISES:

1. **Tu vas souvent au parc avec lui, mais tu ne vas pas au parc avec moi.**
2. **Tu ne vas pas souvent au magasin, mais je vais au magasin tous les jours.**
3. **Ils vont à la plage avec leurs parents.**
4. **Ma fille travaille au magasin avec ses amis.**
5. **Est-ce que tes sœurs vont souvent au centre commercial avec toi ?**
6. **Oui, je mange avec mes sœurs au centre commercial toutes les semaines.**
7. **Nous buvons souvent de l'eau parce que nous avons soif.**
8. **Nous avons vos livres.**
9. **Elle achète de la nourriture au magasin parce que nous n'avons pas de nourriture.**
10. **Tu vas souvent au centre commercial avec leurs amis et eux, mais tu ne vas pas souvent au centre commercial avec nos amis.**

Answers on page 259.

LESSON 110

NEW WORD   **école**

MEANING   *school*

PRONUNCIATION TIP: In the word **école**, notice the accent over the first letter (this is called an *acute accent*). Ordinarily, the letter **e** would sound like the *e* in *bed*. But with the acute accent over it, the first *e* sounds like the *ay* in *bay*. Therefore, **école** sounds something like *ay-coal*.

École, our new word for this lesson, is feminine.

In English, we often do not use an article before the word *school*, like this:

I am going to school.

But in French, you must use an article in front of the word **école**.

Je vais à l'école (*I am going to school*).

Later, we will see the same thing with phrases like *to work, at work, to church*, and *at church*. These English phrases don't require an article, but their French counterparts do. Generally speaking, the French language requires articles before nouns more often than English does.

EXERCISES:
1. **Je vais à l'école tous les jours.**
2. **Nous allons à l'école avec nos amis tous les jours.**
3. **Mon chien va souvent à l'école avec moi.**
4. **Il va au magasin parce que son chat n'a pas de nourriture.**
5. **Elle va à la plage avec lui toutes les semaines.**
6. **Les enfants sont à l'école avec leurs amis.**
7. **Votre chien va toujours à l'école avec les enfants.**
8. **Les chats boivent de l'eau et mangent de la nourriture tous les jours.**
9. **Le chat mange mon livre !**
10. **Mon frère parle français et anglais parce qu'il travaille à la banque.**

Answers on page 259.

LESSON 111

NEW WORD   **je vois**

MEANING   *I see*

The verb **je vois** is an irregular verb. That means that its endings do not fit the expected pattern. You must simply memorize its various forms.

	SINGULAR	PLURAL
FIRST PERSON	**je vois**	**nous voyons**
SECOND PERSON	**tu vois**	**vous voyez**
THIRD PERSON	**il/elle voit**	**ils/elles voient**

EXERCISES:

1. **Je vois souvent la voiture.**
2. **Nous voyons notre mère au parc tous les jours.**
3. **Vous allez au magasin tous les jours parce que vous achetez de la nourriture tous les jours.**
4. **Les enfants voient leurs amis à l'école tous les jours.**
5. **Vous voyez mon frère au centre commercial toutes les semaines.**
6. **Tu travailles avec nous tous les jours.**
7. **Nous allons toujours à la plage avec eux.**
8. **Je ne vais pas au magasin avec toi parce que je ne veux pas de nourriture.**
9. **Est-ce que ton père va à la banque tous les jours ?**
10. **Oui, parce que mon père travaille à la banque.**

Answers on page 259.

LESSON 112

DIRECT OBJECTS

A direct object is a noun that is the target of the action being performed by the subject of the sentence. Here is an example:

> Harold plays the drums.

In this sentence, the word *drums* is the direct object. Here is another example:

> Helen ate the orange.

In this sentence, the word *orange* is the direct object. See if you can find the direct object in each of the exercises below:

EXERCISES:

1. Mr. Jones bought a newspaper.
2. I will see a movie tomorrow.
3. Harry is playing the trombone.
4. On Saturday, we will play baseball.
5. James caught a fish.
6. They accidentally broke the radio.
7. Y'all painted the wrong building.
8. Yesterday we listened to a long speech.
9. Mr. Underwood lost his wallet.
10. Geraldine saw a deer in the woods.

Answers on page 260.

LESSON 113

DIRECT OBJECT PRONOUNS

In the last lesson, we learned that the direct object is the word that is the target of the action being performed by the subject of the sentence.

We wanted to talk about direct objects because they relate directly to the way we use pronouns in French. As we learned recently when studying stressed pronouns, not every pronoun can play the same role in a sentence. We must use different kinds of pronouns to play different roles in a particular sentence.

This isn't something that only happens in French. We do the same thing in English, too. Here's an example:

He sees Mr. Smith at the store every week.

In that sentence, the speaker is using a pronoun to talk about someone seeing Mr. Smith. Since the pronoun is the subject of the sentence, the speaker uses the word *he*. After all, it would be grammatically wrong to say "*Him* sees Mr. Smith at the store every week." Here's another example:

Mr. Smith sees him at the store every week.

Here the speaker is again using a pronoun, this time to talk about the person being seen by Mr. Smith. In this sentence, the pronoun is the direct object, so the speaker uses the word *him* as the pronoun, not the word *he*. After all, it would be grammatically wrong to say "Mr. Smith sees *he* at the store every week."

So, before we finish up this lesson, take a moment to think about the different pronouns we use in English. To help you do that, here is a chart of the different pronouns in English and how they are used.

	SINGULAR	PLURAL
FIRST PERSON	subject: *I* direct object: *me*	subject: *we* direct object: *us*
SECOND PERSON	subject: *you* direct object: *you*	subject: *you (y'all)* direct object: *you (y'all)*
THIRD PERSON	subject: *he, she, it* direct object: *him, her, it*	subject: *they* direct object: *them*

Think about which pronouns you would use for the subject of a sentence, and which pronouns you would use for the direct object of a sentence.

LESSON 114

DIRECT OBJECT PRONOUNS (THIS TIME IN FRENCH)

In the past couple of lessons, we learned about direct objects and direct object pronouns. We learned that in English, when a pronoun is a direct object, you can't use forms such as *I, we, he, she,* or *they*. Instead, you must use forms such as *me, us, him, her,* and *them*.

Well, the same thing happens in the French language. Pronouns such as **je, tu, il, elle, nous, vous, ils,** and **elles** can only be used as the subject of a sentence, not as direct objects. And you can't use stressed pronouns such as **moi** or **toi** as direct objects, either. Instead, you must use special pronouns called *direct object pronouns*. This means that you must become familiar with some more pronouns!

Here are the direct object pronouns in a handy chart.

	Singular	Plural
First Person	**me**	**nous**
Second Person	**te**	**vous**
Third Person	**le/la**	**les**

As you examine these pronouns, notice that you have seen several of these words before. **Nous** and **vous** were both subject pronouns and stressed pronouns. Previously, you have seen **le/la** and **les** used as articles, but here we are seeing those same words in a new role as pronouns. **Me** and **te** are new words that you haven't seen before.

In a French sentence, these direct object pronouns require a different word order than you would expect in a corresponding English sentence. In English, you might have a sentence like this:

I see you.

150

Notice that in this example, the word *you* comes after the verb *see*. But in French, the direct object pronoun would come before the verb, like this:

Je te vois.

A word-for-word translation would be *I you see.*

But what if you wanted to negate this sentence? In other words, what if you wanted to say *I do not see you*? This sentence would be worded like this:

Je ne te vois pas.

Notice that in this kind of sentence, the word **ne** is placed before the direct object pronoun.

EXERCISES:

1. **Tu me vois.**
2. **Je te vois.**
3. **Il ne la voit pas.**
4. **Elle le voit.**
5. **Ils nous voient.**
6. **Nous vous voyons.**
7. **Nous ne les voyons pas.**
8. **Je les vois souvent.**
9. **Nous la voyons souvent.**
10. **Je ne vous vois pas souvent.**

Answers on page 260.

LESSON 115

NEW WORDS   **ne…jamais**

MEANING   *never*

In English, it only takes one word to say *never*. Observe the following sentence:

I <u>never</u> speak French.

But in French, it takes two words to say *never*. Along with the word **jamais**, you must also use the word **ne**. Observe:

Je <u>ne</u> parle <u>jamais</u> français *(I never speak French).*

This is the same type of sentence construction you would use when using **ne…pas** except that you put the word **jamais** where the word **pas** is supposed to go.

By itself, the word **jamais** means something like *ever*. But with the word **ne** negating it, it means *not…ever*, or more simply, *never*.

EXERCISES:

1. **Je ne vais jamais au magasin, mais mes parents vont au magasin toutes les semaines.**
2. **Est-ce que tu vas souvent à la plage ?**
3. **Non, je ne vais jamais à la plage.**
4. **Nous allons souvent au centre commercial, mais nous n'avons jamais d'argent.**
5. **Nous allons à l'école tous les jours.**
6. **Je ne les vois jamais au parc.**
7. **Elles te voient souvent avec tes amis à la plage.**
8. **Mes amis n'ont pas d'argent, mais j'ai cinq dollars.**
9. **Il ne va jamais au parc avec ses chats.**
10. **Nous allons à la plage avec eux toutes les semaines.**

Answers on page 260.

LESSON 116

MEANING   *without*

After the word **sans**, you can have a noun without any kind of article before it. Here's an example:

sans argent *(without money)*

Therefore, in an example like this one, you don't need to have **de** or **de l'** before the word **argent**.

EXERCISES:

1. **Ils ne vont jamais au centre commercial sans argent.**
2. **Nous n'allons jamais au parc sans eau.**
3. **Elle ne va jamais au centre commercial sans toi.**
4. **Les femmes parlent toujours français.**
5. **Mon frère et ses amis vont toujours avec moi à la plage.**
6. **Je te vois avec tes amies tous les jours.**
7. **Nos enfants ne vont jamais à l'école sans leurs livres.**
8. **Ton chat me voit, mais il ne voit pas mon chien.**
9. **Est-ce que tu vois souvent l'amie de ma mère ?**
10. **Oui, je la vois avec ses amies toutes les semaines.**

Answers on page 261.

EXPRESSIONS FRANÇAISES

English speakers say *let's go* all the time. The French have a similar saying.

Allons-y !

Allons-y sounds something like *alloh-zee*. This expression is made up of two parts. You already know that **allons** is the first person plural form of the verb **je vais** which means *I go*. But the part you haven't seen yet is a very important word (comprised of just one letter) that you will need to know when you talk about going places: **y**. **Y** means *there* and is pronounced *ee*.

In English, when we say *let's go*, we don't specify exactly where we are going. In other words, there is no destination mentioned. But in French, you can't do that. Whenever you use the forms of **je vais**, you must give some kind of destination. Observe this incorrect sentence:

Je vais tous les jours *(I go every day).*

You can't say a sentence like that because it does not give a destination. And that's where **y** comes in. To make the sentence correct, all you have to do is add **y** before the verb, and then you have a destination.

J'y vais tous les jours *(I go there every day).*

Notice that **y** is typically placed before the verb—but when it is part of a command, as it is in the expression **allons-y**, the **y** is attached to the end of the verb with a hyphen.

LESSON 117

NEW WORD   **travail**

MEANING   *job, work*

PRONUNCIATION TIP: The "careful" rule that we discussed earlier would suggest that the *l* at the end of **travail** is pronounced. But this is an exception to that rule. When you see the combination of letters *-ail* at the end of a word, it is pronounced like the English word *eye*. Therefore **travail** sounds something like *tra-veye*.

We already have used **je travaille** as a verb, but in French there is also the word **travail** which is a noun. **Travail** is masculine, and can mean either *job* or *work* depending on the context.

Remember that phrases like *to school, at school, to work,* and *at work* require an article in French, but not in English.

EXERCISES:

1. **Je vais au travail tous les jours.**
2. **Je veux un travail.**
3. **Mon père va au travail tous les jours.**
4. **Mon fils veut un travail parce qu'il veut une voiture.**
5. **Ma sœur a des chiens, mais elle n'a pas de chat.**
6. **Je te vois souvent parce que nous mangeons avec toi toutes les semaines.**
7. **Est-ce que ton frère a un travail ?**
8. **Oui, il a toujours de l'argent parce qu'il travaille à la banque.**
9. **Elle ne va jamais à la plage sans ses chiens.**
10. **Elle va toujours au centre commercial avec moi.**

Answers on page 261.

LESSON 118

REVIEW OF PRONOUNS

Over the course of this book we have studied several sets of pronouns. Let's take a few moments now to review each kind of pronoun.

The first pronouns we studied were called *subject pronouns*. You only use these pronouns if the pronoun is the subject of the sentence. We didn't learn these all at once—instead, we learned them one at a time with the various forms of **je suis**. Here are the subject pronouns all in one chart.

	SINGULAR	PLURAL
FIRST PERSON	**je**	**nous**
SECOND PERSON	**tu**	**vous**
THIRD PERSON	**il/elle**	**ils/elles**

For the sake of review, here are some sentences that use each of the subject pronouns.

> **Je veux une voiture** *(I want a car)*.
> **Tu as un livre** *(You have a book)*.
> **Il a trois enfants** *(He has three children)*.
> **Elle a deux frères** *(She has two brothers)*.
> **Nous mangeons de la dinde** *(We are eating some turkey)*.
> **Vous voulez un chat** *(Y'all want a cat* (OR, using formal speech) *You want a cat)*.
> **Ils travaillent au magasin** *(They work at the store)*.
> **Elles vont à la banque** *(They are going to the bank)*.

Once we had a good grasp of subject pronouns, we talked about prepositions. We learned that when a pronoun is the object of a preposition, it can't be a subject pronoun—instead it must be a stressed pronoun.

Here are the stressed pronouns all in one chart.

	SINGULAR	PLURAL
FIRST PERSON	**moi**	**nous**
SECOND PERSON	**toi**	**vous**
THIRD PERSON	**lui/elle**	**eux/elles**

For the sake of review, here are some sentences that use each of the stressed pronouns.

> **Mon chien est au parc avec moi** (*My dog is at the park with me*).
> **Les enfants vont au magasin avec toi** (*The children are going to the store with you*).
> **Ils sont toujours à la plage avec lui** (*They are always at the beach with him*).
> **Elles mangent avec elle au centre commercial toutes les semaines** (*They eat with her at the mall every week*).
> **Nous allons souvent au magasin avec vous et vos parents** (*We often go to the store with y'all and y'all's parents* (OR, using formal speech) *We often go to the store with you and your parents*).
> **Tu ne vas jamais au centre commercial sans eux** (*You never go to the mall without them*).
> **Madame Jones mange souvent avec elles** (*Mrs. Jones often eats with them*).

Finally, we studied direct objects. We learned that if the direct object in a sentence is a pronoun, you can't use a subject pronoun or stressed pronoun—instead you must use yet another kind of pronoun called a *direct object pronoun*.

Here are the direct object pronouns all in one chart.

	SINGULAR	PLURAL
FIRST PERSON	**me**	**nous**
SECOND PERSON	**te**	**vous**
THIRD PERSON	**le/la**	**les**

For the sake of review, here are some sentences that use each of the direct object pronouns.

Ma sœur me voit toutes les semaines *(My sister sees me every week)*.

Les enfants te voient tous les jours *(The children see you every day)*.

Nous ne le voyons pas à la plage, mais nous voyons souvent son fils à la plage *(We do not see him at the beach, but we often see his son at the beach)*.

Ma sœur la voit souvent au parc *(My sister sees her often at the park)*.

Ils ne nous voient jamais à la banque parce que nous n'avons pas d'argent *(They never see us at the bank because we do not have any money)*.

Nous les voyons toujours à la plage parce que nous allons à la plage tous les jours *(We always see them at the beach because we go to the beach every day)*.

Je ne les vois jamais au centre commercial *(I never see them at the mall)*.

LESSON 119

famille

MEANING   *family*

PRONUNCIATION TIP: The word **famille** sounds vaguely like *fah–mee*. And, depending on how fast the speaker is talking, you may also hear a light *yuh* sound at the very end of the word.

Famille is a feminine noun.

EXERCISES:

1. **Ma famille est à la plage.**
2. **Mon frère va au parc avec sa famille toutes les semaines.**
3. **Ma famille mange avec moi tous les jours.**
4. **J'ai un travail et une voiture.**
5. **Elle va au travail tous les jours.**
6. **Ma famille ne va jamais au parc sans nos chiens.**
7. **Est-ce que tu es au magasin avec les enfants ?**
8. **Ils me voient à la banque toutes les semaines.**
9. **Nous les voyons souvent avec leurs enfants au parc.**
10. **Tu vas au centre commercial avec eux toutes les semaines.**

Answers on page 261.

LESSON 120

INFINITIVES

An infinitive is the word *to* plus a verb. Here are some examples of infinitives:

> to walk
> to eat
> to run
> to be

Let's examine some of the different ways infinitives are used:

> I like <u>to sing</u>.
> I want <u>to be</u> a teacher.
> <u>To eat</u> a watermelon is sheer delight.
> I am unable <u>to finish</u> my homework.
> I want <u>to play</u> checkers.

Try to locate the infinitive in each of the exercises below. But be careful! A few of the exercises do not have infinitives. Can you tell which ones they are?

EXERCISES:

1. I do not like to wash the dishes.
2. They want to play a different game.
3. I went to the store.
4. Charles wants to be a policeman.
5. To forgive is divine.
6. She wants to return that sweater to the store.
7. Jenny would like to play the clarinet.
8. We will not go to the party.
9. She will go to the furniture store to buy a chair.
10. Throw the ball to Jeremy.

Answers on page 262.

LESSON 121

NEW WORD   **parler**

MEANING   *to speak*

PRONUNCIATION TIP: The *r* at the end of **parler** is silent, so **parler** sounds something like *par-lay*. In French, verbs that end in *-er* don't follow the "careful" rule that we mentioned earlier in the book.

In English, it takes two words to express an infinitive: the word *to* and a verb. In French, however, it only takes one word to express an infinitive.

In this lesson, we are learning our first French infinitive: the word **parler**. Examine the ending of the word **parler**. Instead of ending in *-e*, *-es*, *-ons*, or some other personal ending, it ends in *-er*. Let's use **parler** in a sentence:

Je veux parler français *(I want to speak French)*.

In the following exercises, get some practice working with the infinitive **parler**. In the next lesson we will continue learning about French infinitives and how they can be used in sentences.

EXERCISES:

1. **Je veux parler français avec mes amis à l'école.**
2. **Ils veulent parler anglais.**
3. **Nous ne voulons pas parler français avec toi.**
4. **Elle veut parler anglais avec son frère.**
5. **Il ne veut pas parler anglais—il veut parler français.**
6. **Ma famille ne va jamais à la plage sans eau.**
7. **Mes amies me voient au centre commercial toutes les semaines.**
8. **Je vais à la plage avec eux.**
9. **Est-ce que tu veux parler français avec moi ?**
10. **Je suis au magasin parce que j'achète de la nourriture.**

Answers on page 262.

161

LESSON 122

MORE ABOUT INFINITIVES

In the last lesson you learned your first French infinitive which was **parler**. But **je parle** isn't the only French verb that has an infinitive—every verb has one. So now that you have been introduced to infinitives, and you have a little experience working with them, it's time to learn the infinitive forms of the other verbs you know. For practice, let's use each one in a sentence.

Je suis means *I am*. It is the verb of being or existing. The infinitive form is **être**, which means *to be*. It sounds something like *eh-truh*. Here is a sentence that uses the infinitive **être**.

Mon chat veut être un chien *(My cat wants to be a dog)*.

J'ai means *I have*. The infinitive form is **avoir** which means *to have*. It sounds something like *ah-vwar*. Here is a sentence that uses the infinitive **avoir**.

Je veux avoir un chien *(I want to have a dog)*.

J'achète means *I buy*. The infinitive form is **acheter** which means *to buy*. It sounds something like *ah-shuh-tay* or simply *ahsh-tay*. Here is a sentence that uses the infinitive **acheter**.

Ma sœur veut acheter une voiture *(My sister wants to buy a car)*.

Je mange means *I eat*. The infinitive form is **manger** which means *to eat*. It sounds something like *mah-zhay*. Here is a sentence that uses the infinitive **manger**.

Mon chat veut manger notre nourriture *(My cat wants to eat our food)*.

Je bois means *I drink*. The infinitive form is **boire** which means *to drink*. It sounds something like *bwar*. Here is a sentence that uses the infinitive **boire**.

Mon chien veut boire de l'eau *(My dog wants to drink some water)*.

Je travaille means *I work*. The infinitive form is **travailler** which means *to work*. It sounds something like *trav-eye-yay*. Here is a sentence that uses the infinitive **travailler**.

> **Les amis de mon frère veulent travailler à la banque** *(My brother's friends want to work at the bank)*.

Je vais means *I go*. The infinitive form is **aller** which means *to go*. It sounds something like *ah-lay*. Here is a sentence that uses the infinitive **aller**.

> **Nous voulons aller au centre commercial** *(We want to go to the mall)*.

Je vois means *I see*. The infinitive form is **voir** which means *to see*. It sounds something like *vwar*. Here is a sentence that uses the infinitive **voir**.

> **Je veux voir mes amis** *(I want to see my friends)*.

In this lesson we have thrown a lot of new words at you—the infinitive of each verb. Keep on memorizing these infinitives, and read the practice sentences in this lesson repeatedly until you are comfortable with all the infinitives. In the next lesson we will learn more about how infinitives function in French grammar.

LESSON 123

USING INFINITIVES

In lesson 90, we talked about a very important subject: verb stems. We observed that each form of a verb starts with the same few letters, and this part of the verb is called the *stem* of the verb. This is a very important point to understand in your quest to learn the French language.

But for students of French, the infinitive is very important to know about because the stem comes from the infinitive form of the verb. To find the stem of any French verb, take the infinitive and remove the final two letters. For example, with the verb **je parle**, the infinitive form of the verb is **parler**. So, take the infinitive...

parler

And then remove the last two letters, leaving this:

parl-

Now, you have the verb stem, and that's a very useful thing to have. *If the verb is a regular verb*, (this is very important) you can take the verb stem and then add the personal endings to make the various present tense forms of the verb. Just for the sake of review, here are those endings again.

	SINGULAR	PLURAL
FIRST PERSON	**-e**	**-ons**
SECOND PERSON	**-es**	**-ez**
THIRD PERSON	**-e**	**-ent**

Let us repeat that *this only works with regular verbs*. If a verb is irregular, each form is different and they won't follow a pattern. Actually, most of the verbs in this book are irregular. But there are many regular French verbs out there!

Even though many of the verbs in this book are irregular, we still want you to have the knowledge and training to be able to find a verb's stem and add the personal ending on your own. So let's practice this method once, and try to form the six present forms of a regular verb.

To do this we will need a regular verb. Let's pick one that we know. The verb **je parle** is a regular verb, so let's use that one.

First, let's take the infinitive:

parler

And then remove the last two letters, leaving this:

parl-

Now let's add the personal endings.

	SINGULAR	PLURAL
FIRST PERSON	**parl + e = parle**	**parl + ons = parlons**
SECOND PERSON	**parl + es = parles**	**parl + ez = parlez**
THIRD PERSON	**parl + e = parle**	**parl + ent = parlent**

As you can see, this system allows us to make all six present tense forms of a regular verb. For verbs that end in -er, the endings are always the same (with the exception of the irregular verb **aller**). As we learned earlier, **aller** has four irregular forms that don't follow any predictable pattern.

Sometimes, the stem of a verb may not be the same for every form, but the endings are still the same, as with the verb **acheter**. In the singular forms and in the third person plural, there is an additional accent mark over the e. But the verb **acheter** still contains the same endings that all -er verbs have.

LESSON 124

NEW WORD   **vêtements**

MEANING   *clothes*

The word **vêtements** is plural. The singular form of **vêtements** is **vêtement**, which means *item of clothing*, but we won't be using the singular form. Instead we will use the plural form of the word, along with an indefinite article, to mean *clothes* or *clothing*.

EXERCISES:

1. **Je veux acheter des vêtements.**
2. **Nous achetons des vêtements au magasin.**
3. **Ils veulent avoir un chat, mais leur père ne veut pas avoir de chat.**
4. **Est-ce que ta sœur a un travail ?**
5. **Non, mais ma sœur veut travailler à la banque.**
6. **La famille de monsieur Jones va souvent à la plage.**
7. **Je veux aller au magasin, mais je n'ai pas ma voiture.**
8. **Je veux boire de l'eau parce que j'ai soif.**
9. **Nous n'allons jamais à la plage sans toi.**
10. **Je veux voir mes amis au centre commercial.**

Answers on page 262.

LESSON 125

NEW WORD **aujourd'hui**

MEANING *today*

PRONUNCIATION TIP: This word sounds something like *oh-zhore-dwee*.

EXERCISES:

1. **Je veux acheter des vêtements aujourd'hui.**
2. **Nous ne voulons pas manger de dinde aujourd'hui.**
3. **Tu veux aller à la plage aujourd'hui avec les enfants.**
4. **Mes amis veulent aller au centre commercial aujourd'hui, mais ils n'ont pas de voiture.**
5. **Elles veulent acheter des vêtements aujourd'hui, mais elles n'ont pas d'argent.**
6. **Est-ce que vous allez souvent au centre commercial avec votre famille ?**
7. **Non, nous n'allons jamais au centre commercial.**
8. **Notre chien veut être à la plage.**
9. **Mes amis me voient à l'école tous les jours.**
10. **Ma sœur veut acheter une voiture parce que son fils veut une voiture.**

Answers on page 263.

LESSON 126

MEANING   *I need*

In English, when we want to say that we need something, we use the verb *need*. But in French, this kind of statement is worded differently. In French, if you wanted to say *I need a car*, literally you would word it like this: *I have need of a car.*

Let's learn to say this in French. First, you'll need to say **j'ai** *(I have)*. Here are the forms of **j'ai**, just for review:

	SINGULAR	PLURAL
FIRST PERSON	**j'ai**	**nous avons**
SECOND PERSON	**tu as**	**vous avez**
THIRD PERSON	**il/elle a**	**ils/elles ont**

Next, you'll need the word **besoin**, which means *need*.

    j'ai besoin *(I have need)*

Then, throw in the word **de**, which means *of*.

    j'ai besoin de *(I have need of)*

The final ingredient is the thing you need.

    J'ai besoin de la voiture *(I have need of the car).*

A word-for-word translation would read *I have need of the car*. But we will translate this kind of expression into English as *I need the car.*

If you want to negate this statement and say *I do not need the car*, here is how you would do it:

Je n'ai pas besoin de la voiture *(I do not have need of the car).*

A word-for-word translation would read *I do not have need of the car*. But we will translate this kind of expression into English as *I do not need the car.*

Voiture is a feminine noun—here's an example with needing a masculine noun:

J'ai besoin du livre *(I need the book).*

In that example, notice that **de** and **le** combined into **du.** Here's an example with an indefinite article:

J'ai besoin d'une voiture *(I need a car).*

Notice that in that example, there was elision between **de** and **une**. Here's that same sentence negated:

Je n'ai pas besoin d'une voiture *(I do not need a car).*

You can also use **j'ai besoin** with an infinitive, like this:

J'ai besoin d'aller au centre commercial *(I need to go to the mall).*

In that example, the infinitive **aller** started with a vowel, so there was elision between **de** and **aller.**

One last thing before we go on to the exercises. With food-related words, we often use the partitive article like this:

J'ai de la dinde *(I have some turkey).*

But with the expression **j'ai besoin de**, you would not use the partitive article. Observe:

J'ai besoin de dinde *(I need turkey).*
J'ai besoin d'eau *(I need water).*

If you want to say that you do not need some of an uncountable thing, like food or money, the sentence construction is the same, but you negate the verb **j'ai**, like this:

> **Je n'ai pas besoin de dinde** *(I don't need (any) turkey).*
> **Je n'ai pas besoin d'eau** *(I don't need (any) water).*

EXERCISES:

1. **Ma famille a besoin d'une voiture.**
2. **J'ai besoin de boire de l'eau parce que j'ai soif.**
3. **Mon papa a besoin d'acheter de la nourriture.**
4. **Ils ont besoin d'aller au magasin parce qu'ils ont besoin d'acheter des vêtements.**
5. **Nous voulons aller à la plage aujourd'hui.**
6. **Mes parents veulent avoir un chien.**
7. **La fille veut aller au centre commercial avec ses amis.**
8. **Les enfants veulent manger au centre commercial, mais nous n'avons pas faim.**
9. **Vous ne voulez jamais aller à la plage.**
10. **Mes amis ne me voient jamais sans livre.**

Answers on page 263.

EXPRESSIONS FRANÇAISES

What's the thing that gets you out of bed in the morning? The thing that gives you a sense of purpose, or a reason to live? Whatever it is, it's your **raison d'être**.

The word **raison** means *reason*. **D'être** is a combination of **de** and **être**. As you already know, **de** means *of* and **être** is an infinitive which means *to be*. In French, an infinitive can function the way a gerund functions in English, so you could translate **être** as *being*. Therefore, **raison d'être** literally means *reason of being* or, as we might say in English, *reason to live*.

LESSON 127

NEW WORD **demain**

MEANING *tomorrow*

EXERCISES:

1. J'ai besoin d'aller à la banque demain.
2. Nous voulons aller à la plage aujourd'hui.
3. Elle veut aller au magasin demain, mais nous avons besoin d'acheter de la nourriture aujourd'hui.
4. J'ai besoin d'aller au centre commercial parce que ma fille a besoin d'acheter des vêtements.
5. Est-ce que vous avez une famille, monsieur Smith ?
6. Ils ont besoin de manger de la nourriture parce qu'ils ont faim.
7. Elle veut parler français avec moi, mais je ne parle pas français.
8. Je ne veux pas aller au magasin avec eux aujourd'hui.
9. Mes amis me voient souvent au magasin.
10. Mes hommes ne travaillent jamais sans nourriture.

Answers on page 263.

LESSON 128

NEW WORD   **je peux**

MEANING   *I am able, I can*

In French, we use the verb **je peux** to say that we are able to do something. But **je peux** cannot do anything by itself. It needs an infinitive to complete its meaning. Observe the following examples:

Je peux travailler (*I am able to work* OR *I can work*).

Je peux aller au magasin (*I am able to go to the store* OR *I can go to the store*).

Je ne peux pas acheter de vêtements (*I am not able to buy clothes* OR *I cannot buy clothes*).

In each of these examples, **je peux** worked with an infinitive to show what activity the subject of the sentence was or was not able to do. When an infinitive plays this role in a sentence it is called a *complimentary infinitive*.

EXERCISES:

1. **Je peux aller au parc.**
2. **Je peux parler français, mais je ne peux pas parler anglais.**
3. **Je peux aller au parc demain.**
4. **Je ne peux pas acheter de voiture aujourd'hui.**
5. **Je ne peux pas travailler avec toi tous les jours.**
6. **Nous voulons acheter des vêtements aujourd'hui.**
7. **Il n'a pas besoin d'acheter de vêtements, mais il veut aller au centre commercial.**
8. **Je veux voir mes amis.**
9. **Est-ce que vous avez des enfants ?**
10. **Nous n'allons jamais à la plage sans nos chiens.**

Answers on page 264.

LESSON 129

THE OTHER FORMS OF JE PEUX

Now it's time to learn the other forms of **je peux**, since **je peux** is only the first person singular form of the verb. The infinitive form of this verb is **pouvoir**, which means *to be able*.

Here are all the forms of **je peux/pouvoir** in a handy chart:

	SINGULAR	PLURAL
FIRST PERSON	**je peux**	**nous pouvons**
SECOND PERSON	**tu peux**	**vous pouvez**
THIRD PERSON	**il/elle peut**	**ils/elles peuvent**

EXERCISES:

1. **Tu ne peux pas aller à la banque parce que tu n'as pas de voiture.**
2. **Elle peut acheter une voiture parce qu'elle travaille à la banque.**
3. **Nous pouvons aller au parc, mais nous ne pouvons pas aller à la plage.**
4. **Est-ce que tu peux aller au magasin avec moi demain ?**
5. **Il ne peut pas acheter de vêtements sans argent.**
6. **Nous avons besoin d'un chien.**
7. **Je ne peux pas aller au centre commercial aujourd'hui, mais je peux aller au centre commercial demain.**
8. **Est-ce que vous voulez aller au centre commercial ?**
9. **Vous voyez madame Jones toutes les semaines à la banque.**
10. **Nous n'allons pas à la plage sans voiture.**

Answers on page 264.

LESSON 130

NEW WORD   **je porte / porter**

MEANING   *I carry / to carry*

PRONUNCIATION TIP: Remember, infinitives that end in *-er* do not follow the "careful" rule. Therefore **porter** would sound something like *por-tay*.

Now that you are familiar with infinitives, whenever we give you a new verb, we will give you both the first person singular form and the infinitive form. For example, in this lesson, we are giving you both **je porte** and its infinitive form **porter**.

Je porte/porter is a regular verb. Here are its six present tense forms.

	Singular	Plural
First Person	**je porte**	**nous portons**
Second Person	**tu portes**	**vous portez**
Third Person	**il/elle porte**	**ils/elles portent**

EXERCISES:

1. **Je porte mes livres à l'école tous les jours.**
2. **Nous portons toujours de la nourriture et de l'eau au parc.**
3. **Mes parents portent toujours de l'argent.**
4. **Elle ne peut pas aller à la plage demain.**
5. **Notre chien a faim.**
6. **Il a soif, mais il ne veut pas boire d'eau.**
7. **Mon chien n'a pas besoin de vêtements.**
8. **Je peux travailler à la banque, mais je ne peux pas travailler au magasin.**
9. **Nous ne pouvons pas aller au centre commercial avec eux aujourd'hui parce que je veux voir ma sœur et ses enfants.**
10. **Votre ami me voit souvent à la banque.**

Answers on page 264.

LESSON 131

NEW WORD   **je lis / lire**

MEANING   *I read / to read*

This new verb is irregular, so its forms must be memorized.

	SINGULAR	PLURAL
FIRST PERSON	**je lis**	**nous lisons**
SECOND PERSON	**tu lis**	**vous lisez**
THIRD PERSON	**il/elle lit**	**ils/elles lisent**

Earlier, we mentioned that when you say that you speak a particular language, you don't need to put an article in front of the name of the language, like this:

    Je parle français.

In other words, there is no **le** before the word **français** in that sentence. But when you say that you *read* a language, you do need to put a definite article in front of the name of the language that you are reading, like this:

    Je lis le français.

EXERCISES:

1. **Je lis deux livres toutes les semaines.**
2. **Est-ce que tu veux lire un livre ?**
3. **Nous ne voulons pas lire de livre aujourd'hui.**
4. **Elles lisent toujours des livres à l'école.**
5. **Tu peux lire le français, mais tu ne peux pas parler français.**

6. **Tu as besoin d'aller à l'école demain.**
7. **Nous portons nos livres à l'école tous les jours.**
8. **Mes fils ne veulent pas travailler aujourd'hui, mais ils peuvent travailler demain.**
9. **Je veux acheter des vêtements, mais nous ne voulons pas aller au centre commercial avec toi.**
10. **Je te vois souvent au parc avec ta famille.**

Answers on page 265.

LESSON 132

NEW WORD   **journal**

MEANING   *newspaper*

PRONUNCIATION TIP: The *l* at the end of **journal** is not silent, so **journal** will sound something like *zhor-nal.*

The word **journal** is masculine.

The plural form of **journal** is not **journals**. Most of the time, to make a French noun plural we just add an *s*. But the rules are different for nouns that end in *-al*, such as **journal**. To make a noun that ends in *-al* plural, the ending changes to *-aux*. Therefore the plural form of **journal** is **journaux**. The *x* in **journaux** is silent, so **journaux** sounds something like *zhor-no.*

EXERCISES:

1. **Je veux lire le journal.**
2. **Mes parents lisent le journal tous les jours.**
3. **J'ai un travail—je porte les journaux tous les jours.**
4. **Ma mère lit le journal avec mon père tous les jours.**
5. **Est-ce que vous allez à la plage avec votre famille toutes les semaines ?**
6. **Je ne veux pas aller à l'école aujourd'hui.**
7. **Nous avons besoin de boire de l'eau tous les jours.**
8. **Ils achètent des vêtements au centre commercial, mais nous travaillons à l'école.**
9. **Elle ne peut pas voir ses amies aujourd'hui, mais elle peut aller au centre commercial demain.**
10. **Elles veulent manger de la dinde parce qu'elles ont faim, mais nous n'avons pas de dinde.**

Answers on page 265.

LESSON 133

NEW WORD   **église**

MEANING   *church*

PRONUNCIATION TIP: Since the first *e* in **église** has an acute accent mark over it, it will sound like *ay*. Therefore, **église** will sound something like *ay-gleez*.

Église is feminine.

EXERCISES:

1. **Il va à l'église toutes les semaines.**
2. **Mes enfants vont à l'église avec moi demain.**
3. **Est-ce que vous allez à l'église toutes les semaines ?**
4. **Nous ne pouvons pas aller à l'église parce que nous n'avons pas de voiture.**
5. **Vous portez les journaux à l'école tous les jours.**
6. **Je ne peux pas manger de dinde, mais je peux manger du riz.**
7. **Monsieur Jones ne va jamais à l'église, mais nous allons à l'église toutes les semaines.**
8. **Est-ce que tu veux lire le journal aujourd'hui ?**
9. **Mon chien veut aller à l'école avec moi aujourd'hui.**
10. **Ils ont besoin d'acheter des vêtements parce qu'ils vont à l'école demain.**

Answers on page 265.

LESSON 134

NEW WORD   **bibliothèque**

MEANING   *library*

PRONUNCIATION TIP: The word **bibliothèque** has four syllables. It sounds something like *bee-blee-yoh-teck*.

Bibliothèque is feminine.

EXERCISES:

1. **Je veux lire des livres, mais je ne peux pas aller à la bibliothèque parce que je n'ai pas de voiture.**
2. **Ma sœur lit le journal tous les jours, mais je ne lis jamais le journal.**
3. **Est-ce que tu veux aller à la bibliothèque ?**
4. **Est-ce que vous voulez aller à la bibliothèque ?**
5. **Non, je ne veux pas lire de livres aujourd'hui, mais je peux aller à la bibliothèque avec toi demain.**
6. **Nous n'allons jamais à l'église, mais nous avons besoin d'aller à l'église toutes les semaines.**
7. **Mes chiens ne peuvent pas lire le journal.**
8. **Il porte toujours un journal, mais je porte toujours deux journaux.**
9. **Le chien a le journal de mon père !**
10. **Je vais à la bibliothèque parce que je veux lire les livres et aussi les journaux.**

Answers on page 266.

LESSON 135

In everyday conversation, we often tell others the reason why we are doing something. Observe the following example:

I am going to the mall <u>for the purpose of</u> buying clothes.

That sentence was a little wordy, wasn't it? We could say the same thing in a shorter way, using an infinitive, like this:

I am going to the mall <u>to buy</u> clothes.

In that example, we used an infinitive to express purpose—to communicate to someone the reason for our trip to the mall. Think about this for a moment, and in the next lesson, we will study how to express purpose in French.

EXPRESSIONS FRANÇAISES

When you present something to someone, you can add excitement by saying **voilà** at the moment of presentation.

Voilà is a combination of two words that eventually got smashed together into one word. The first part is **voi-**, which comes from the verb **voir** which means *to see*. The second part is **là** (notice the accent mark over the letter *a*), which means *there*. So, **voilà** literally means *see there*.

LESSON 136

EXPRESSING PURPOSE IN FRENCH

In this lesson, we will learn how to express purpose in French. To accomplish this, we will use the infinitive, accompanied by a helping word.

The helping word that we need for expressing purpose is **pour**. The word **pour** is often translated into English as *for*, but **pour** can be used in different ways. In this lesson, we will be using the word **pour** to mean *for the purpose of* or *in order to*.

Here's an example of using the word **pour** plus an infinitive to express purpose.

> **Je vais au magasin pour acheter de la nourriture** (*I am going to the store to buy food*).

In this sentence, the speaker uses the word **pour** to communicate that he or she is going to the store for a certain purpose, and then uses the infinitive **acheter** to show what that purpose is—in this case, to buy something.

EXERCISES:

1. **Mes parents vont souvent au centre commercial pour acheter des vêtements.**
2. **Il va à la bibliothèque pour lire les journaux.**
3. **Elle va au magasin pour acheter de la nourriture.**
4. **Je vais au centre commercial toutes les semaines pour voir mes amis.**
5. **Ils vont à l'église toutes les semaines.**
6. **Vous ne pouvez pas acheter de voiture.**
7. **Elles ont besoin d'aller au magasin pour acheter de la nourriture.**
8. **Je porte mes livres à l'école tous les jours.**
9. **Est-ce que tu vas à la banque demain ?**
10. **Non, je vais à la banque aujourd'hui parce que j'ai besoin d'argent.**

Answers on page 266.

LESSON 137

NEW WORD   **restaurant**

MEANING   *restaurant*

PRONUNCIATION TIP: The *t* at the end of the word **restaurant** is silent, so it sounds something like *re-stoh-rah*.

Restaurant, our new word for this lesson, is masculine.

EXERCISES:

1. **Nous allons au restaurant pour manger toutes les semaines.**
2. **Je vais souvent au restaurant pour manger avec mes amis.**
3. **Est-ce que tu veux aller au restaurant pour manger ?**
4. **Oui ! Je veux manger parce que j'ai faim !**
5. **Nous ne pouvons pas aller au restaurant aujourd'hui parce que nous n'avons pas d'argent.**
6. **Est-ce que tu veux aller à la bibliothèque aujourd'hui ?**
7. **Non, je ne peux pas aller à la bibliothèque aujourd'hui, mais je peux aller à la bibliothèque demain.**
8. **Monsieur Jones va à l'église avec sa famille toutes les semaines.**
9. **Mon fils porte les journaux tous les jours parce qu'il a besoin d'argent.**
10. **Mon père ne peut pas aller au travail aujourd'hui parce qu'il n'a pas de voiture.**

Answers on page 266.

LESSON 138

NEW WORD **je déjeune / déjeuner**

MEANING *I have lunch / to have lunch*

PRONUNCIATION TIP: Notice the acute accent over the second letter of **dé-jeune**, which gives that *e* an *ay* sound. Therefore **déjeuner** sounds something like *day-zhuh-nay*.

Je déjeune is a regular verb. Observe the different forms of this verb in the following chart.

	SINGULAR	PLURAL
FIRST PERSON	**je déjeune**	**nous déjeunons**
SECOND PERSON	**tu déjeunes**	**vous déjeunez**
THIRD PERSON	**il/elle déjeune**	**ils/elles déjeunent**

Here are two example sentences which use the verb **je déjeune**.

Nous déjeunons tous les jours au restaurant (We have lunch every day at the restaurant).
Je veux déjeuner (I want to have lunch).

The word **déjeuner**, which is the infinitive form of **je déjeune**, can also be a noun that means *lunch*. You can use the noun **déjeuner** the same way you would use the word *lunch* in English.

Le chat mange mon déjeuner ! (*The cat is eating my lunch!*)

183

EXERCISES:

1. **Nous déjeunons tous les jours.**
2. **Mes amis déjeunent avec moi.**
3. **Est-ce que tu veux déjeuner avec moi aujourd'hui ?**
4. **Je ne peux pas déjeuner avec toi aujourd'hui, mais je peux déjeuner demain.**
5. **Tu as besoin de déjeuner.**
6. **Elle déjeune avec ses parents tous les jours.**
7. **Je veux aller au restaurant avec toi pour déjeuner.**
8. **Ma sœur va à la bibliothèque pour lire des livres.**
9. **Nous ne pouvons pas acheter de voiture parce que nous n'avons pas d'argent.**
10. **Mes parents lisent le journal, mais ils ont besoin d'aller à l'église.**

Answers on page 267.

LESSON 139

NEW WORDS **tous les matins**

MEANING *every morning*

The word **matin** means *morning*. It is masculine. This word is part of the new expression we are learning in this lesson, **tous les matins**, which means *every morning*.

In addition to **tous les matins**, you might also want to know how to say *this morning*, which is **ce matin**.

EXERCISES:

1. **Je vais à la plage tous les matins.**
2. **Je ne veux pas travailler ce matin.**
3. **Ma famille déjeune tous les jours.**
4. **Ma sœur va à l'école tous les matins.**
5. **Mon père lit le journal tous les matins.**
6. **Est-ce que vous allez souvent à la plage avec votre famille ?**
7. **Non, nous n'allons jamais à la plage, mais nous allons souvent au parc.**
8. **Je bois de l'eau tous les matins.**
9. **Mon fils ne veut pas aller à l'école ce matin.**
10. **Ils ne peuvent pas lire le livre parce qu'ils sont enfants.**

Answers on page 267.

LESSON 140

NEW WORDS   **petit déjeuner**

MEANING   *breakfast*

PRONUNCIATION TIP: The *t* at the end of the word **petit** is silent.

You already know that the French word for lunch is **dejeuner**. In this lesson, we are going to learn the French word for *breakfast*, which is closely related to the word for *lunch*. In fact, the French word for *breakfast* is simply the word **dejeuner** with the word **petit** before it (**petit** means *little*). Therefore, the French term for *breakfast* is **petit dejeuner**.

It's kind of a long story, but we aren't going to learn a verb that means *to have breakfast* as we did with **déjeuner**. Instead, we will have a slightly different sentence structure for talking about the action of having breakfast. Here is a word-for-word translation of the kind of sentence structure we will be using:

> I take the breakfast.

In this sentence, we are using the word *take* to mean *eat*. To say sentences like this in French, you will need to learn the French verb for *take*, which is **je prends** (the infinitive form is **prendre**). Use the chart below to familiarize yourself with the different forms of **je prends/prendre** (it's an irregular verb).

	SINGULAR	PLURAL
FIRST PERSON	**je prends**	**nous prenons**
SECOND PERSON	**tu prends**	**vous prenez**
THIRD PERSON	**il/elle prend**	**ils/elles prennent**

Here are some examples of sentences which use this verb. Notice that before **petit déjeuner** we will be using a definite article.

186

Je prends le petit déjeuner.

Literally, this sentence says *I am taking the breakfast*, but we translate it simply as *I am having breakfast.* Here's another example:

Je prends le petit déjeuner tous les jours.

Literally, this sentence says *I take the breakfast all the days*, but we translate it as *I have breakfast every day.* One last example:

Je veux prendre le petit déjeuner.

Notice that **prendre** here is an infinitive. Literally, this sentence says *I want to take the breakfast* but we translate it as *I want to have breakfast.*

EXERCISES:

1. **Ma famille prend le petit déjeuner tous les matins.**
2. **J'ai besoin de prendre le petit déjeuner, mais nous n'avons pas de nourriture.**
3. **Est-ce que tu veux prendre le petit déjeuner avec moi ce matin ?**
4. **Tes parents ne vont jamais au restaurant pour manger.**
5. **Il veut aller au restaurant pour déjeuner.**
6. **Je veux acheter une voiture, mais je n'ai pas d'argent.**
7. **Je porte mon déjeuner avec moi à l'école tous les jours.**
8. **Nous allons à la bibliothèque demain pour lire des livres.**
9. **Ma mère veut aller au magasin pour acheter un journal.**
10. **Vous ne pouvez pas aller au centre commercial aujourd'hui parce que vous n'avez pas d'argent.**

Answers on page 267.

LESSON 141

NEW WORD   **maintenant**

MEANING   *now*

PRONUNCIATION TIP: **Maintenant** sounds something like *met-nah* or *meh-teh-nah*, depending on how fast the speaker is talking.

EXERCISES:

1. **Je veux aller à la plage maintenant.**
2. **Je veux déjeuner maintenant parce que j'ai faim !**
3. **Mes chiens veulent manger maintenant.**
4. **Elle veut lire son journal tous les jours.**
5. **Je veux aller au centre commercial maintenant pour acheter des vêtements.**
6. **Est-ce que tu peux aller au centre commercial avec moi ?**
7. **Nous lisons nos livres tous les matins à l'école.**
8. **Les enfants ont faim et ils veulent prendre le petit déjeuner maintenant.**
9. **Est-ce que tu vas au restaurant pour déjeuner ?**
10. **Non, je vais à la bibliothèque maintenant pour voir mes amis.**

Answers on page 268.

EXPRESSIONS FRANÇAISES

The joy of being alive is the **joie de vivre**. This is a simple expression: **joie** means *joy*. **De**, as you already know, means *of*. **Vivre** is an infinitive which means *to live* or *living*. So, **joie de vivre** means *joy of living*.

LESSON 142

NEW WORDS   **tous les soirs**

MEANING   *every evening, every night*

The masculine French noun **soir** means *evening*, but it can also mean *night*.

If you have a French sentence that uses the word **soir** to talk about something happening at 7:00 PM, in that case you might translate the word **soir** into English as *evening*. On the other hand, if you have a French sentence that uses the word **soir** to talk about something happening at 10:00 PM, you might translate the word **soir** as *night*.

In addition to **tous les soirs**, you might also want to know the expression **ce soir**, which means *this evening* or *tonight*.

EXERCISES:

1. **Elles vont au restaurant pour manger tous les soirs.**
2. **Je veux aller au restaurant ce soir.**
3. **Nous voulons déjeuner maintenant parce que nous avons faim.**
4. **Monsieur Smith porte toujours son journal au parc.**
5. **Est-ce que nous pouvons aller au centre commercial pour acheter des vêtements ce soir ?**
6. **Non, mais tu peux aller à la bibliothèque pour lire tes livres.**
7. **Il ne va jamais à l'école sans ses livres.**
8. **Nous voyons nos amis à l'église toutes les semaines.**
9. **Est-ce que tu veux aller à la plage ce matin ?**
10. **Le chien mange notre petit déjeuner !**

Answers on page 268.

LESSON 143

NEW WORD   **je dîne / dîner**

MEANING   *I have dinner / to have dinner*

PRONUNCIATION TIP: **Dîner** ends with an *r*, but does not follow the "careful" rule we mentioned earlier because it is an infinitive that ends in *-er*. Therefore **dîner** sounds vaguely like *dee-nay.*

The way we talk about the evening meal in French is similar to the way we talk about lunch. We have the word **dîner**, which is both a noun and a verb.

As a noun, **dîner** is masculine and means the evening meal, which, depending on your preference, you may call *dinner* or *supper*. As a verb, we have **je dîne**, and the infinitive form is **dîner**. It means *to have dinner* or *to have supper*. See the chart below for all the present tense forms of **je dîne/dîner.**

	SINGULAR	PLURAL
FIRST PERSON	**je dîne**	**nous dînons**
SECOND PERSON	**tu dînes**	**vous dînez**
THIRD PERSON	**il/elle dîne**	**ils/elles dînent**

EXERCISES:

1. **Le chat mange ton dîner !**
2. **Je dîne avec ma famille tous les soirs.**
3. **Ils vont au restaurant pour dîner tous les soirs.**
4. **Ma sœur dîne avec moi toutes les semaines.**
5. **Nous déjeunons à l'école tous les jours.**
6. **Elle veut prendre le petit déjeuner avec ses amis tous les matins.**
7. **Est-ce que tu veux aller à la bibliothèque pour lire des livres ?**

8. Non, je ne peux pas aller à la bibliothèque parce que j'ai besoin d'aller à la plage avec mes amis.
9. Tu ne peux pas prendre le petit déjeuner ce soir, mais tu peux dîner.
10. Aujourd'hui nous prenons le petit déjeuner à l'église.

Answers on page 268.

LESSON 144

NEW WORD   **sur**

MEANING   *on*

The preposition **sur** means *on*. But to use the word **sur**, we need some furniture to put things on—so along with the word **sur**, let's learn two new nouns. The noun **table** isn't hard to remember because it's spelled the same as its English translation, *table*. The word **table** is feminine. The word **bureau** means *desk*, but it can also mean *office*. The word **bureau** is masculine.

To make the plural form of **bureau**, you need to learn a new rule. When a word ends in *-eau*, we don't add an *s*. Instead, we add the letter *x*. Therefore, the plural form of **bureau** is **bureaux**. The *x* in **bureaux** is silent, so **bureaux** sounds the same as **bureau**.

EXERCISES:

1. **Ton déjeuner est sur la table.**
2. **Le journal de mon père est sur son bureau.**
3. **Le chat est sur la table !**
4. **Tes amis sont à la plage, mais tu es à la bibliothèque.**
5. **Nous n'avons pas besoin de deux bureaux.**
6. **J'ai besoin de lire le journal.**
7. **Les enfants portent leurs livres à l'école tous les jours.**
8. **Nous ne pouvons pas déjeuner parce que nous n'avons pas de nourriture.**
9. **Je veux aller à la bibliothèque maintenant pour lire des livres.**
10. **Est-ce que tu prends le petit déjeuner tous les matins ?**

Answers on page 269.

LESSON 145

REVIEW OF PLURAL FORMS

By this point in the book, you have had experience with all the different ways to make French nouns plural. Let's review the rules here.

For a noun that does not end in -s, make it plural by adding an s.

voiture ⟶ voitures

If a noun already ends with the letter s, don't add another—just leave it as it is. The singular form and the plural form are the the same, and you must use the context to figure out whether it is singular or plural.

fils ⟶ fils

If a noun ends in -al, make it plural by changing the ending to -aux.

journal ⟶ journaux

If a noun ends in -eau, make it plural by adding an x.

bureau ⟶ bureaux

EXERCISES:

1. **J'ai un fils, mais tu as deux fils.**
2. **Ma mère lit deux journaux tous les matins.**
3. **Au travail, j'ai deux bureaux.**
4. **Est-ce que vous avez un journal ?**
5. **Oui—j'ai trois journaux.**
6. **Les journaux sont sur la table.**
7. **J'ai besoin de boire de l'eau parce que j'ai soif.**
8. **Nous avons deux bureaux.**
9. **Mon frère ne peut pas travailler aujourd'hui.**
10. **Au restaurant, ils prennent le petit déjeuner tous les matins et ils dînent tous les soirs.**

Answers on page 269.

LESSON 146

NEW WORD   **dans**

MEANING   *in*

The word **dans** means *in.*

EXERCISES:

1. **Ma famille est dans la voiture.**
2. **Les livres sont dans notre bureau.**
3. **Nous sommes à la bibliothèque.**
4. **Je veux être à la plage, mais je suis au travail.**
5. **Tes chats veulent manger maintenant.**
6. **Nous avons besoin d'acheter de la nourriture ce soir.**
7. **Ils ont besoin de dîner parce que leurs enfants ont faim.**
8. **Ils vont au magasin demain pour acheter de la nourriture.**
9. **Nous ne pouvons pas aller à l'église aujourd'hui parce que nous n'avons pas de voiture.**
10. **Ton dîner est sur la table.**

Answers on page 269.

LESSON 147

NEW WORDS   **maison / salon**

MEANING   *house / living room*

PRONUNCIATION TIP: When there is a single *s* between two vowel sounds, the *s* is pronounced like a *z*. Therefore **maison** sounds something like *meh-zoh*.

Maison, the new word for this lesson, is feminine. **Salon** is masculine.

The French expression **à la maison** literally means *to the house* or *at the house*. But this expression is often used to express the thought of *at home* or *home*, as we see in these English sentences:

> I am <u>at home</u>.
> I am <u>home</u>.
> I am going <u>home</u>.

Notice that the first two examples above were identical in meaning, whether or not the word *at* is included in the sentence.

Now let's examine those same sentences expressed in French.

> **Je suis à la maison** *(I am at home)*.
> **Je suis à la maison** *(I am home)*.
> **Je vais à la maison** *(I am going home)*.

Again, notice that the first two sentences were identical, and in your English translation you can choose whether to include or leave out the word *at*.

EXERCISES:

1. **Le chien est dans la maison.**
2. **Les chats sont dans le salon.**
3. **Mon frère va à la maison demain.**

195

4. **Nous ne pouvons pas dîner sans table.**
5. **Ma mère n'est pas à la maison aujourd'hui.**
6. **Nous mangeons toujours de la nourriture au parc.**
7. **Vos chiens sont dans le salon sur la table !**
8. **Mon frère ne peut pas aller à l'école aujourd'hui, mais il peut aller à l'école demain.**
9. **Je ne veux pas lire de livre aujourd'hui.**
10. **Elle veut dîner au restaurant ce soir.**

Answers on page 270.

LESSON 148

NEW WORDS   **cuisine / salle à manger**

MEANING   *kitchen / dining room*

The word **cuisine**, which means *kitchen*, is feminine. So is **salle à manger**, which means *dining room*.

EXERCISES:

1. **La nourriture est dans la cuisine.**
2. **La table est dans la salle à manger.**
3. **Les journaux sont dans le salon, sur le bureau.**
4. **Les filles veulent aller au centre commercial pour voir leurs amis et aussi pour acheter des vêtements.**
5. **Nous ne pouvons pas dîner sans table.**
6. **Tu es toujours à la bibliothèque, mais tu ne lis jamais les livres.**
7. **Mon papa veut son journal, mais le journal n'est pas sur son bureau.**
8. **Nous n'avons pas de table dans notre cuisine, mais nous avons une table dans la salle à manger.**
9. **Nous avons besoin d'aller au magasin pour acheter une table, mais nous n'avons jamais d'argent.**
10. **Mon père ne veut pas aller au travail aujourd'hui—il veut aller à la maison.**

Answers on page 270.

LESSON 149

MEANING   *bedroom / bed*

Chambre is feminine, and **lit** is masculine.

As you might have noticed, the French word **chambre** looks similar to our English word *chamber*. In everyday speech, however, **chambre** just means *bedroom*. The word **chambre** can also refer to a hotel room. To specify a bedroom, you could use the longer term **chambre à coucher**, but it's more common to just say **chambre**.

The English expression *in bed* translates into French as either **au lit** or **dans le lit**. Each of these has a slightly different meaning. If somebody is **au lit**, he or she is *in bed*, either asleep or resting. If somebody is **dans le lit**, he or she is physically *in bed*, but not necessarily asleep—the person could just be reading or watching television.

Au lit is only for people—therefore, if your dog or cat has jumped up onto your bed for a nap, the French way to express that would be **dans le lit**. When referring to an animal, **dans le lit** is probably best translated into English as *on the bed*.

EXERCISES:

1. **Ma sœur est dans sa chambre.**
2. **Les chats sont dans mon lit.**
3. **Est-ce que les enfants sont au lit ?**
4. **Les chiens sont dans le lit avec mes parents.**
5. **Mon lit et mon bureau sont dans ma chambre.**
6. **Mes frères et mes sœurs sont dans la maison.**
7. **La chambre de mon frère a deux lits.**
8. **Mon père et ma mère sont dans la cuisine, mais ma sœur est dans la salle à manger.**
9. **Ton petit déjeuner est sur la table dans la salle à manger.**
10. **Je ne vais jamais à l'école sans mes livres.**

Answers on page 270.

LESSON 150

NEW WORD   **je dors / dormir**

MEANING   *I sleep / to sleep*

The verb **je dors/dormir** is irregular.

In the previous lesson, we learned about the difference between **au lit** and **dans le lit**. However, that rule only applies to the verb **je suis**. With the verb **je dors/dormir**, it is already implied that you are asleep. So, we simply use **dans le lit**.

	SINGULAR	PLURAL
FIRST PERSON	**je dors**	**nous dormons**
SECOND PERSON	**tu dors**	**vous dormez**
THIRD PERSON	**il/elle dort**	**ils/elles dorment**

EXERCISES:

1. **Je dors dans mon lit tous les soirs.**
2. **Nous ne voulons pas manger maintenant—nous voulons dormir !**
3. **Les chats dorment dans le salon tous les soirs.**
4. **Je ne veux pas aller à la plage maintenant—je veux dormir dans mon lit.**
5. **Les chats dorment dans le lit avec les enfants tous les soirs.**
6. **Mon chien dort toujours dans le lit avec moi.**
7. **Il dort dans sa chambre.**
8. **Les livres sont sur le bureau.**
9. **Vos amis sont dans la maison, dans le salon.**
10. **Nous ne prenons jamais le petit déjeuner.**

Answers on page 271.

LESSON 151

NEW WORD   **je fais / faire**

MEANING   *I do / to do, I make / to make*

The irregular verb **je fais/faire** is a very versatile word in French. It can mean *to do* or *to make.* You must use the context of the sentence to determine the best translation.

	SINGULAR	PLURAL
FIRST PERSON	**je fais**	**nous faisons**
SECOND PERSON	**tu fais**	**vous faites**
THIRD PERSON	**il/elle fait**	**ils/elles font**

When it comes to food, you can use **je fais/faire** to talk about preparing a meal. When you say that you are preparing one of the three meals of the day (breakfast, lunch, or dinner), put the definite article in front of the name of the meal, like this:

Je fais le dîner *(I am making dinner).*

When it comes to doing work, you can also use **je fais/faire** to talk about doing a job, like this:

Je fais toujours mon travail *(I always do my job).*

As usual, the context of the sentence will tell you the intended meaning.

EXERCISES:

1. **Elle fait le déjeuner tous les jours.**
2. **Nous faisons le petit déjeuner maintenant.**

3. **Je prends le petit déjeuner tous les matins, mais tu ne prends jamais le petit déjeuner.**
4. **Est-ce qu'ils font le petit déjeuner tous les matins ?**
5. **Je fais mon travail tous les jours, mais tu dors toujours.**
6. **Ils font toujours le dîner.**
7. **Nous faisons le dîner dans la cuisine, mais nous dînons dans la salle à manger.**
8. **Mon chien dort toujours dans la cuisine, mais son lit est dans le salon.**
9. **Le livre est dans le bureau.**
10. **Tu as besoin d'aller au centre commercial pour acheter des vêtements.**

Answers on page 271.

LESSON 152

MORE ABOUT POUR

We already learned to use **pour** to express purpose. But the word **pour**, however, can also mean *for* in the sense of *for the benefit of*, like this:

Je fais le déjeuner pour mes parents (*I am making lunch for my parents*).

EXERCISES:

1. **Je fais le dîner pour mes amis toutes les semaines.**
2. **Je veux faire le déjeuner pour mes amis.**
3. **Mon père ne veut pas acheter de voiture pour mon frère.**
4. **Mon frère fait le dîner pour ses enfants.**
5. **Les enfants sont au lit maintenant.**
6. **Est-ce que ta mère fait le dîner ce soir ?**
7. **Nous ne pouvons pas prendre le petit déjeuner parce que les enfants dorment.**
8. **Je dors toujours dans ma chambre.**
9. **Ma famille dîne dans la salle à manger.**
10. **Nous achetons un chien pour les enfants, mais mon mari veut un chat.**

Answers on page 271.

EXPRESSIONS FRANÇAISES

Vive la France ! is an expression of patriotic fervor that means something like *May France live!* or *Long live France!*

As you already know, **la** is a definite article. In French, the definite article is used in places where it would not be used in English. So here, we have **la** before the word **France**.

In French, all nouns are assigned genders, even countries! The word **France** is a feminine noun, so it will have the feminine definite article **la**.

The verb here, **vive**, is a form of the verb **vivre** which means *to live*. **Vive** is a special kind of verb called a *subjunctive* verb. If you continue to study French beyond this book, and we hope you will, you will learn much more about subjunctive verbs.

We use subjunctive verbs in English, too, often expressed with words like *let* or *may*. In this particular context, the subjunctive is expressing the action that you wish for or desire to happen. For example, what if you went to your grandmother's birthday party and said to her, "Grandma, may you live to be 100 years old!" Then, you would be expressing a wish or desired action. Here, the words *may you live* form a subjunctive verb. This is only one of several uses of the subjunctive.

And this is the kind of role the verb **vive** plays in the expression **vive la France**. **Vive** means *may it live*. As a subjunctive verb, it expresses the wish that France prosper and thrive.

Here's another similar French expression. See if you can translate it on your own:

> **Vive la liberté !**

LESSON 153

NEW WORD   **j'aime / aimer**

MEANING   *I like / to like*

Our new verb for this lesson, **j'aime/aimer**, is a regular verb.

	SINGULAR	PLURAL
FIRST PERSON	**j'aime**	**nous aimons**
SECOND PERSON	**tu aimes**	**vous aimez**
THIRD PERSON	**il/elle aime**	**ils/elles aiment**

If you want to say that you like a particular thing, such as a certain cat, you can make a statement like this:

J'aime le chat *(I like the cat).*

This statement means that there is a particular cat that you like. But if you want to say that you like cats in general, you would not say it like this incorrect example:

J'aime chats.

That would be wrong. Instead, you would use a plural definite article and a plural noun, like this:

J'aime <u>les</u> chats *(I like cats).*

Of course, when you translate a sentence like this into English, you wouldn't translate **les** into anything.

If the thing you like is an uncountable item, like rice, you might say this:

J'aime le riz *(I like rice)*.

And finally, you can say that you like to do a certain action, using an infinitive, like this:

J'aime aller à la plage *(I like to go to the beach)*.

EXERCISES:

1. **Ma fille aime le chien.**
2. **Ma fille aime les chiens.**
3. **Mon père n'aime pas les chats.**
4. **Est-ce que tu aimes lire ?**
5. **Oui, je lis deux livres toutes les semaines.**
6. **Je n'aime pas mon travail.**
7. **Nous aimons la maison parce que la maison a une salle à manger et aussi un salon.**
8. **Je ne peux pas dormir parce que je n'aime pas mon lit.**
9. **J'aime faire le petit déjeuner pour ma famille tous les matins.**
10. **Nous avons une table dans notre cuisine.**

Answers on page 272.

LESSON 154

MORE ABOUT GENDER

In this book we have taught you that the French language has two genders: masculine and feminine. But other languages such as German, Russian, Latin, ancient Greek, etc. have a third gender in addition to masculine and feminine. This gender is called *neuter*. The word *neuter* is a Latin word that means *neither*. Neuter words are neither masculine nor feminine. The word *neuter* is related to other words such as *neutral* and *neutron*.

Let's talk about English for a moment. In English, we have three genders: masculine, feminine, and neuter. For example, the pronoun *he* is masculine, *she* is feminine, and *it* is neuter (neither masculine nor feminine). In English, the neuter pronoun *it* is used for non-living objects because they don't have a gender.

Since there is no neuter gender in French, there is no neuter pronoun that corresponds to the English pronoun *it*. Instead, you have to pick either a masculine or feminine pronoun such as **il** or **elle**. This might take some getting used to as an English speaker. Here's an example to show you what we mean, using the new word **jolie** which means *pretty*.

> **Est-ce que tu aimes ma voiture ?** (*Do you like my car?*)
> **Oui. J'aime ta voiture parce qu'elle est jolie** (*Yes. I like your car because it (she) is pretty.*)

Notice that in the second sentence, we translated the French pronoun **elle** into English as *it*, because in English a car does not have a gender—it's neuter.

This same concept holds true with direct object pronouns. Observe the following English sentence:

I want it.

To translate that thought into French, you would need to pick either a masculine direct object pronoun or a feminine direct object pronoun to represent the word *it*. The direct object pronouns in French which could be translated as *it* are **le** and **la**. Therefore, if the thing you want is a masculine noun, you would say this:

206

Je le veux *(I want it).*

But if the thing you want is feminine, you would say this:

Je la veux *(I want it).*

If the French verb starts with a vowel, there will be elision between the direct object pronoun and the beginning of the verb, like this:

Je l'achete *(I am buying it).*

In that case, whether the direct object pronoun is **le** or **la**, it still ends up being **l'** because of the elision between the direct object pronoun and the next word. Therefore, this type of construction will look the same for both genders.

LESSON 155

MORE ABOUT J'AIME/AIMER

A couple of lessons ago, we talked about **j'aime/aimer**, and how it means *to like*. But that's not the only meaning this verb can have. Depending on the context, this verb can also mean *to love*.

Here is the difference: when you talk about things or animals, **j'aime/aimer** means *like*. But when you are talking about a person, **j'aime/aimer** means *love*. This love can be romantic love (that is, to be in love with someone) or familial love, depending on the context.

We already covered this, but as a reminder, here's an example of **j'aime/aimer** expressing *like*.

> **J'aime la plage** *(I like the beach)*.

Here's an example of **j'aime/aimer** expressing romantic *love*.

> **J'aime ma femme** *(I love my wife)*.

Here's an example of **j'aime/aimer** expressing familial *love* for a family member.

> **Je t'aime, maman** *(I love you, Mom)*.

EXERCISES:

1. **Il aime les chiens.**
2. **J'aime mon mari.**
3. **Nous aimons lire.**
4. **J'aime manger au restaurant tous les soirs.**
5. **J'aime Michael.**
6. **Il n'aime pas travailler.**
7. **Il ne veut pas travailler maintenant—il veut dormir.**
8. **Il fait le petit déjeuner dans la cuisine.**
9. **La nourriture est sur la table dans le salon.**
10. **Ils aiment la maison parce qu'elle a quatre chambres.**

Answers on page 272.

LESSON 156

NEW WORDS   **pain / œuf**

MEANING   *bread / egg*

PRONUNCIATION TIP: **Pain** sounds like *peh*, with a nasal vowel. The word **œuf** follows the "careful" rule, so it sounds something like *uff*. But when the word **œuf** is plural (that's **œufs**) both the *f* and the *s* become silent. Therefore, **œufs** sounds something like the *oo* in *good*.

Both of our new words for this lesson are masculine.

Now that you know a couple of food words, we would like to show you yet another way to use the word **pour**. You can use it to talk about having a certain food for a certain meal, like this:

> **Je mange toujours des œufs <u>pour</u> le petit déjeuner** *(I always eat eggs for breakfast).*

EXERCISES:

1. **J'aime les œufs.**
2. **Ma mère aime le pain.**
3. **Vous aimez manger des œufs.**
4. **Est-ce que les œufs sont dans la cuisine ?**
5. **Nous avons besoin d'acheter des œufs et du pain demain.**
6. **Nous ne pouvons pas aller au centre commercial parce que nous déjeunons maintenant.**
7. **J'aime ma femme et elle m'aime aussi.**
8. **Nous mangeons des œufs pour le petit déjeuner tous les matins.**
9. **Je n'aime pas dormir dans le salon—j'aime dormir dans ma chambre, dans mon lit.**
10. **Elle n'aime pas la maison parce qu'elle n'a pas trois chambres.**

Answers on page 272.

LESSON 157

NEW WORDS   **pain grillé / beurre**

MEANING   *toast / butter*

PRONUNCIATION TIP: The acute accent at the end of the word **grillé** gives the *e* an *ay* sound. Therefore, **grillé** sounds something like *gree-yay*. **Beurre** has one syllable and sounds something like *behr*.

In the last lesson, you learned the word for *bread*. To say *toast* in French, the expression is **pain grillé**, which literally means *grilled bread.*

Pain grillé and **beurre** are both masculine.

EXERCISES:

1. **Est-ce que tu veux du pain grillé et du beurre ?**
2. **J'aime le pain grillé sans beurre.**
3. **Ma sœur aime manger du pain grillé et du beurre pour le petit déjeuner tous les matins.**
4. **Est-ce que vous voulez du pain et du beurre ?**
5. **Ils aiment manger des œufs et du pain grillé tous les matins.**
6. **Vous ne pouvez pas acheter de vêtements au centre commercial sans argent.**
7. **Ma mère fait le petit déjeuner ce matin.**
8. **Le chien dort dans mon lit.**
9. **Mes parents sont dans la cuisine.**
10. **Les enfants ne sont pas à la maison maintenant.**

Answers on page 273.

LESSON 158

NEW WORDS **je fais la cuisine / faire la cuisine**

MEANING *I cook / to cook*

Sometimes in English, you hear people say things such as *I like to cook* or *my husband loves to cook*. In French, this kind of statement would be worded like this: *I like to do the cooking* or *my husband loves to do the cooking*.

You already know the word **cuisine**. A few lessons ago, we learned that it means *kitchen*. But the word **cuisine** can also mean *cooking*. We have borrowed the French word **cuisine** into English as a fancy word for *food*.

You already know the verb **je fais/faire** which means *to do* or *to make*.

Let's put it all together. Observe this example sentence:

J'aime faire la cuisine.

Literally, this sentence says *I like to do the cooking*. This translates pretty well into English most of the time, but sometimes it might sound better to translate **faire la cuisine** simply as *to cook*. The context of the sentence will help you figure out the best way to translate **faire la cuisine**. When you do the exercises, just translate **faire la cuisine** into what sounds best in English.

You would use this expression to talk about cooking in a general way—but you can't use this expression to talk about cooking a specific food.

EXERCISES:

1. **Mon père n'aime pas faire la cuisine.**
2. **Mon mari fait toujours la cuisine.**
3. **Mon frère veut faire la cuisine tous les soirs.**
4. **Je fais la cuisine tous les soirs, mais ce soir je veux aller au restaurant pour dîner.**
5. **Ils ont faim parce qu'ils ne prennent jamais le petit déjeuner.**

6. **Ta nourriture n'est pas sur la table—ta nourriture est sur le bureau.**
7. **Nous sommes dans le salon, mais mes parents sont dans la cuisine.**
8. **Elle fait la cuisine tous les soirs.**
9. **Il ne peut pas faire la cuisine aujourd'hui parce qu'il va au travail.**
10. **Mon lit est dans ma chambre.**

Answers on page 273.

EXPRESSIONS FRANÇAISES

If you're at the mall doing some shopping with friends, you might say something like this: "I'll go to the bookstore while you go shopping for clothes, and we can **rendezvous** back here again at 7:30."

The word **rendezvous**, as used in English, can be either a noun or a verb. You can **rendezvous**, or you can arrange to have a **rendezvous**. In French, it's actually written with a hyphen as **rendez-vous**.

The first part of the word, **rendez**, is a form of the verb **rendre** which means things like *return, deliver, convey,* or *present*. **Rendez** is an imperative verb, which means that it is used to issue a command. **Vous**, as you already know, means *y'all*. In this expression, **vous** is being used as a reflexive pronoun. So, **rendez-vous** literally means something like *present yourselves!* or *convey yourselves!*

LESSON 159

NEW WORDS **céréales / lait**

MEANING *cereal / milk*

Céréales is feminine, and **lait** is masculine.

When you are talking about breakfast cereal, the word **céréales** is always plural. Therefore it will have the plural article **des** before it. Don't ask why—it's complicated. We'll tell you when you're older.

EXERCISES:

1. **Mon frère mange des céréales tous les matins.**
2. **Nous voulons des céréales avec du lait.**
3. **Je veux manger des céréales avec du lait.**
4. **Est-ce que tu prends le petit déjeuner maintenant ?**
5. **Je ne peux pas porter les livres à l'école tous les matins.**
6. **Est-ce que vous voulez boire de l'eau, monsieur Smith ?**
7. **Ma sœur n'aime pas les œufs, mais elle aime les céréales avec du lait.**
8. **Mon père mange du pain grillé et du beurre.**
9. **Je n'aime pas le pain grillé.**
10. **Nous allons au centre commercial pour dîner.**

Answers on page 273.

LESSON 160

NEW WORDS   **plus de**

MEANING   *more*

PRONUNCIATION TIP: In the expression **plus de**, the *s* in **plus** is not silent as you might expect. Therefore, it kind of (sort of) rhymes with the English word *moose*.

When you use the expression **plus de**, you don't need to use an article before the noun that you are saying you want more of. You only use the word **plus** and the word **de**, and then the noun, like this:

Je veux plus de lait (*I want more milk*).
J'ai besoin de plus de livres (*I need more books*).

Remember that if the next word after **de** starts with a vowel, there will be elision, and **de** will shorten to **d'**. For example:

plus d'argent

EXERCISES:
1. **Nous voulons plus de lait.**
2. **J'ai besoin d'aller au magasin parce que nous avons besoin de plus de nourriture.**
3. **Ma famille n'aime pas les œufs.**
4. **J'aime Jennifer.**
5. **Les enfants n'aiment pas les œufs.**
6. **Vous avez besoin de lire plus de livres.**
7. **Mon frère a besoin de boire plus d'eau.**
8. **Le chat est dans la cuisine.**
9. **Je veux manger du pain avec mon déjeuner.**
10. **Ma mère fait le dîner pour mon père.**

Answers on page 274.

LESSON 161

NEW WORDS **s'il vous plaît**

MEANING *please*

S'il vous plaît is an expression that means *please*. It is comprised of several words.

S'il is a contraction of the word **si** and the word **il**. **Si** means *if*. You already know the word **il** because it is a third person singular subject pronoun. Here, the pronoun **il** means *it*. So **s'il** means *if it*.

You already know the word **vous**. It's the second person plural direct object pronoun that means *y'all*. **Plaît** is the third person singular form of the verb **plaire** which means *to please*. Put it all together, and **s'il vous plaît** means *if it pleases you*. But we will translate it into English as *please*.

When we talk to someone using the expression **s'il vous plaît**, it is formal speech because you are using the second person plural pronoun **vous** to address someone. Therefore, if you are speaking with someone you don't know very well, such as a waiter in a restaurant, you would say **s'il vous plaît**. But if you are speaking to a family member or to friends, you could replace **vous** with **te**, which is the second person singular direct object pronoun. That would give you the less formal expression **s'il te plaît**.

EXERCISES:

1. **Je veux des œufs, s'il te plaît.**
2. **Nous voulons manger maintenant, s'il te plaît.**
3. **Est-ce que tu peux faire le petit déjeuner pour moi, s'il te plaît ?**
4. **Plus de pain grillé et de céréales, s'il vous plaît.**
5. **Ils aiment aller à la plage toutes les semaines.**
6. **Est-ce que vous aimez manger des œufs ?**
7. **Ils aiment souvent lire les livres de mon père.**
8. **J'ai besoin de faire le petit déjeuner pour mes enfants.**
9. **Est-ce que tu aimes aller au parc souvent?**
10. **Le chien veut mon dîner.**

Answers on page 274.

LESSON 162

NEW WORD   **j'adore / adorer**

MEANING   *I love / to love, I adore / to adore*

J'adore/adorer is a regular verb. You can use it with either things or people. Before we explain how to use it, take a moment to examine this chart.

	SINGULAR	PLURAL
FIRST PERSON	**j'adore**	**nous adorons**
SECOND PERSON	**tu adores**	**vous adorez**
THIRD PERSON	**il/elle adore**	**ils/elles adorent**

When you use **j'adore/adorer** with things, it means that you love that thing. Here's an example:

> **J'adore le pain** *(I love bread).*

When you use **j'adore/adorer** with people, it means that you feel strong affection or admiration for that person, but does *not* imply romantic love. Therefore, when used with a person, **j'adore/adorer** translates into English the way we would use the word *adore*. Here's an example:

> **J'adore André** *(I adore André).*

So, in the answer key, when **j'adore/adorer** is used with a thing, we will translate it as *love*. But when **j'adore/adorer** is used with a person, we will translate it as *adore*.

216

EXERCISES:

1. **J'adore la plage.**
2. **J'aime la plage.**
3. **Ma sœur adore monsieur Smith.**
4. **Mon fils adore faire la cuisine.**
5. **Mon frère adore aller à la bibliothèque et lire des livres.**
6. **Est-ce que tu peux travailler aujourd'hui ?**
7. **Pour le petit déjeuner, j'adore manger du pain grillé et du beurre.**
8. **Mon père ne peut pas travailler aujourd'hui.**
9. **Elle aime acheter des vêtements au centre commercial.**
10. **Nous allons au restaurant pour dîner.**

Answers on page 274.

LESSON 163

Salade is feminine. **Sandwich** is masculine.

With the word **salade**, you can use both the partitive article and the indefinite article. The partitive article would be used when you are talking about an unspecified quantity of salad, such as when you are eating salad for dinner.

> **Je veux de la salade avec mon dîner** *(I want some salad with my dinner)*.

The indefinite article would be used when you are talking about a pre-packaged salad—that is, a unit of salad that you might buy at the grocery store.

> **Je vais au magasin pour acheter une salade** *(I am going to the store to buy a salad)*.

EXERCISES:

1. **Je veux manger une salade pour le déjeuner.**
2. **Mes amis veulent manger de la salade pour le déjeuner, mais je veux manger un sandwich.**
3. **J'aime les sandwichs.**
4. **J'adore les sandwichs.**
5. **Ma mère fait de la salade pour le déjeuner.**
6. **Mon père mange de la salade avec son dîner.**
7. **Ma sœur veut une voiture.**
8. **Nous allons à la bibliothèque pour lire des livres.**
9. **Elle veut aller à la plage.**
10. **Je t'aime.**

Answers on page 275.

LESSON 164

NEW WORDS   **jus / café**

MEANING   *juice / coffee*

PRONUNCIATION TIP: The *s* in **jus** is silent, so **jus** rhymes with *few*. The sound at the beginning is like the *s* in the word *vision*.

Jus and **café** are both masculine.

In the last lesson, we saw that with the word **salade**, you can use either the partitive article or the indefinite article depending on what kind of salad you are talking about. It's the same deal with the word **café**. For example, **du café** means *coffee* or *some coffee*, but **un café** means *a cup of coffee*.

EXERCISES:

1. **Un café, s'il vous plaît.**
2. **Elle veut du café, mais je veux du jus.**
3. **Plus de jus, s'il vous plaît.**
4. **Mon père fait du café pour ma mère.**
5. **J'adore le café.**
6. **Je ne peux pas dormir parce que je bois du café.**
7. **J'aime boire du café avec mon petit déjeuner.**
8. **Nous buvons du café tous les matins.**
9. **Ma sœur fait le petit déjeuner tous les matins.**
10. **Est-ce que tu aimes ton café avec du lait ?**

Answers on page 275.

LESSON 165

MORE ABOUT DE AND À

So far we have used the word **de** to show possession. In this lesson, we are going to show you a related (but slightly different) way to use **de**. Let's start with an example in English:

apple juice

In this example, we have two nouns next to each another. The first noun, *apple*, is telling us something about the noun that comes after it. In this case, the word *apple* is telling us what the juice is made of. In other words, *apple juice* means *juice made from apples*.

But in French, to say *apple juice*, you would not word it the same way as we would in English. In other words, you would not just put together the French word for *apple* and then the French word for *juice*. Instead, you would need to use the word **de**. Here's an example of how we would express this in French. The French word for *juice* is **jus**, and the French word for *apple* is **pomme**.

jus de pomme

If you translated that example word for word, it would say *juice of apple*. But, of course, we would translate it into English as *apple juice*.

Also, keep in mind that if the next word starts with a vowel, there will be elision between **de** and the next word. For example, *orange juice* would be **jus d'orange**.

What we just showed you is the correct way to talk about foods that are a direct product of another food. For instance, apple juice comes directly from an apple. But if a certain food is just flavored with or partly made with another food (not a direct product of that food) you would word it differently, using the preposition **à**. You already have a lot of experience working with **à**, as in phrases like **à la plage**. But here, it won't really mean *to*. Observe how we would say *turkey sandwich* in French:

sandwich à la dinde

In that example, the preposition **à** doesn't really translate into anything in English. Instead, it just shows that the sandwich has a turkey-ish quality to it, or a turkey-ish characteristic.

The example we just showed you involved a feminine noun, **dinde**. If the second noun is masculine, **a** and **le** will combine into **au**. As an example of this, here's how to say *chicken sandwich* using the masculine noun **poulet**, which means **chicken**.

> **sandwich au poulet**

Here's one final example which is extremely common in Europe.

> **café au lait**

Café au lait is coffee flavored with hot milk, therefore it's **café au lait**, not **café de lait**.

Starting in the next lesson, the exercises will contain foods like these, so you can get some practice working with them.

EXPRESSIONS FRANÇAISES

Have you ever received an invitation that said **RSVP** on it?

The letters **RSVP** stand for the French expression **répondez, s'il vous plaît**. The first word, **répondez**, is a form of the verb **répondre** which means *to reply* or *to answer*. **Répondez** is an imperative verb, which means that it is issuing a command: *reply!*

You already know the rest of the expression, which is **s'il vous plaît**, which simply means *please*.

Therefore, **répondez, s'il vous plaît** means *reply, please* or *respond, please*. So, if you receive an invitation that says **RSVP** on it, it means that the sender would like to know whether or not you are coming to the party!

LESSON 166

NEW WORD   **fruit**

MEANING   *fruit*

PRONUNCIATION TIP: The French word **fruit** has a somewhat strange pronunciation. It sounds something like *frwee*.

Fruit, our new word for this lesson, is masculine. In French, when you refer to *fruit* in a general way, you would use the plural form of **fruit**, which is **fruits**. But even though it is plural in French, you would probably translate it into English as the singular word *fruit*.

As we saw with the word **céréales**, the plural word **fruits** will have the plural article **des** before it.

In addition to the new word for this lesson, remember that you learned a couple of new words in the last lesson. **Pomme** is feminine, and so is **orange**.

EXERCISES:

1. **Nous avons besoin de manger plus de fruits tous les jours.**
2. **J'aime boire du jus d'orange pour le petit déjeuner.**
3. **Mon fils n'aime pas le jus de pomme.**
4. **Les enfants mangent des sandwichs à la dinde.**
5. **Mes enfants adorent le jus d'orange.**
6. **Nous n'avons pas besoin de dormir—nous avons besoin de boire du café parce que nous avons besoin de travailler.**
7. **J'aime manger du pain grillé tous les matins.**
8. **Mon fils aime les sandwichs au poulet.**
9. **Je ne peux pas boire de café, mais j'adore le jus.**
10. **Mes amis vont au parc.**

Answers on page 275.

LESSON 167

NEW WORDS **soupe / fromage**

MEANING *soup / cheese*

Soupe is feminine. You can use either the indefinite or partitive article with **soupe**, just as you can with **café**.

Fromage is masculine, and the indefinite article cannot be used with it. We can still use the definite and partitive articles with **fromage**.

EXERCISES:

1. **Ma mère adore le fromage.**
2. **Je mange un sandwich au fromage.**
3. **Nous allons au restaurant pour manger de la soupe au poulet.**
4. **Il mange de la soupe pour le dîner tous les soirs.**
5. **Je veux boire du jus de pomme et du jus d'orange avec mon petit déjeuner.**
6. **Ma famille adore le pain grillé et le beurre.**
7. **Plus de café, s'il vous plaît.**
8. **Elle ne peut pas aller au parc parce qu'elle déjeune avec sa famille maintenant.**
9. **Mes enfants prennent le petit déjeuner tous les matins avec moi.**
10. **Monsieur Smith veut manger un sandwich à la dinde pour le déjeuner tous les jours, mais madame Smith aime manger des fruits et une salade de poulet.**

Answers on page 276.

LESSON 168

MEANING   *thank you*

In French, **merci** simply means *thank you*. There are several ways to thank people for various things and actions, but in this book we are only going to show you something very simple: how to thank someone for a concrete or tangible object.

If you are thanking someone for a concrete object such as food, a pencil, or a newspaper, you say the word **merci**, then the word **pour**, then the item you are thanking the person for. Here's an example:

> **Merci pour la nourriture** (*Thank you for the food*).

As long as you are learning how to say *thank you* in French, you might as well learn how to say *you're welcome*. One of the most common ways to say *you're welcome* in French is **de rien**.

EXERCISES:

1. **Merci pour le journal.**
2. **De rien.**
3. **Merci pour le fromage, maman.**
4. **De rien, mon fils.**
5. **Merci pour le sandwich à la dinde, papa.**
6. **De rien, ma fille.**
7. **Nous avons besoin de plus de nourriture, s'il vous plaît.**
8. **Mes sœurs n'aiment pas la soupe au poulet.**
9. **Est-ce que tu aimes le jus de pomme ?**
10. **Ce matin, je veux du jus d'orange et aussi des fruits pour le petit déjeuner.**

Answers on page 276.

LESSON 169

NEW WORDS   **légume / pomme de terre**

MEANING   *vegetable / potato*

Légume is masculine, and **pomme de terre** is feminine. You may notice that it takes three words in French to say *potato*. The French word for *potato* literally means *apple of earth*, or *earth apple*.

As we saw with the words **céréales** and **fruits**, we will be using the word **légume** as a plural word, with the article **des** before it.

EXERCISES:

1. **Ma mère fait du poulet, des légumes et des pommes de terre pour le dîner.**
2. **Mon papa adore les pommes de terre.**
3. **Maman, je ne veux pas manger de légumes.**
4. **Mes enfants n'aiment pas les légumes.**
5. **J'aime les sandwichs à la dinde.**
6. **Le restaurant a des soupes, des salades et des sandwichs.**
7. **Aujourd'hui, nous mangeons des fruits pour le petit déjeuner.**
8. **Mon papa veut manger un sandwich au poulet pour le déjeuner, mais je veux de la soupe de poulet.**
9. **Est-ce que tu aimes le jus d'orange ?**
10. **Non, je n'aime pas le jus d'orange, mais j'adore boire du café.**

Answers on page 276.

LESSON 170

NEW WORD   **c'est**

MEANING   *this is / that is / it is*

PRONUNCIATION TIP: **C'est** sounds somewhat similar to the English word *say*.

Waaaaay back in lesson 47 we started introducing you to third person pronouns like **il** and **elle**. And we started giving you exercises like **il est mon père** and **elle est la fille**. But we told you that sentences like these were just for practice working with pronouns because they aren't really the way a native French speaker would talk. But in this lesson we're going to show you a more common way that French speakers speak in the third person.

If you want to say *she is the girl*, instead of using the pronoun **elle** and saying **elle est la fille**, it would be better and more common to say **<u>c'est</u> la fille**. Therefore, in this lesson, let's learn about the expression **c'est** and how to use it.

C'est is comprised of two words. The first word is **ce** which means *this*, *that*, or *it*. You already know the second word, which is **est**. Because of elision, these two words combine to form **c'est**.

There are several ways that you can use **c'est** in a sentence. You can use it to introduce someone, like this:

> **C'est mon ami** *(This/that is my friend)*.

You can also use it to say what something is:

> **C'est ma voiture** *(This/that is my car)*.

You can even use it to ask a question:

> **Est-ce que c'est ton chien ?** *(Is this/that your dog?)*

In order to negate **c'est**, you must split apart **c'est** into **ce** and **est**, and then put **ne** and **pas** around the verb, like this:

Ce n'est pas un livre *(This/that is not a book).*

EXERCISES:

1. **Est-ce que c'est ton père ?**
2. **Oui, c'est mon père.**
3. **Est-ce que c'est ta sœur ?**
4. **Non, ce n'est pas ma sœur.**
5. **Est-ce que c'est du fromage ?**
6. **Non, c'est du jus d'orange.**
7. **C'est un sandwich au fromage.**
8. **J'aime la salade de pommes de terre.**
9. **Ce n'est pas un sandwich au poulet.**
10. **Merci pour la soupe de légumes, maman.**

Answers on page 277.

LESSON 171

NEW WORDS **Qui est-ce ?**

MEANING   *Who is this? / Who is that? / Who is it?*

PRONUNCIATION TIP: **Qui est-ce** sounds something like *key-ess.*

Our new expression for this lesson, **qui est-ce**, is made up of three different words, two of which you already know. **Qui** means *who.* **Est** means *is.* Since **ce** can mean *this, that,* or *it,* **qui est-ce** can mean *who is this?, who is that?,* or *who is it?*

EXERCISES:

1. **Qui est-ce ? Ton papa ?**
2. **Non, c'est mon ami.**
3. **Qui est-ce ? Ton amie ?**
4. **Non, ce n'est pas mon amie. C'est ma sœur.**
5. **Mon frère veut lire des livres à la bibliothèque toutes les semaines.**
6. **Qui est-ce ? Monsieur Smith ?**
7. **Oui, monsieur Smith dîne au restaurant tous les soirs.**
8. **Ma femme adore manger de la salade de poulet pour le déjeuner tous les jours.**
9. **J'aime les sandwichs au fromage.**
10. **J'aime ta sœur.**

Answers on page 277.

LESSON 172

NEW WORDS   **Qu'est-ce que c'est ?**

MEANING   *What is this? / What is that? / What is it?*

PRONUNCIATION TIP: **Qu'est-ce que c'est ?** sounds something like *kess-kuh-say*.

Qu'est-ce que c'est ?, our new phrase for this lesson, may seem intimidating to you at first—like a big jumble of words. But you already know most of the words in this phrase.

At the end of the expression is **c'est**, which you learned two lessons ago. It means *this is*, *that is*, or *it is*.

In the middle of the expression is **est-ce que ?**, which we have been using for many lessons now to introduce questions. Literally, **est-ce que ?** means *is it that?*

At the very beginning of this expression is the word **que**. This French word can have many different meanings. It can mean *that*, as in *is it that* but it can also mean *what* (this is what we call an *interrogative pronoun*). You have seen this word before, with the meaning of *that*, but you have not seen it used to mean *what*. But here, at the beginning of the expression **qu'est-ce que c'est**, we have the word **que** with the meaning of *what*. There is elision between the *e* at the end of **que** and the beginning of the next word, **est**, producing **qu'est**.

So, if you translated it all word for word, **qu'est-ce que c'est** could say things like…

- What is it that this is?
- What is it that that is?
- What is it that it is?

We told you all of that just for educational purposes—so you know how the expression breaks down literally. But when you are translating or using this expression, don't think about each individual word—just remember that this expression means *what is this?*, *what is that?*, or *what is it?*

229

EXERCISES:

1. **Qu'est-ce que c'est ? Un sandwich au poulet ?**
2. **Non, c'est un sandwich à la dinde.**
3. **Qu'est-ce que c'est ? Votre maison ?**
4. **Non, ce n'est pas ma maison. C'est un restaurant !**
5. **Qui est-ce ? Ton fils ?**
6. **Mes enfants adorent le jus de pomme, mais j'aime le jus d'orange.**
7. **Une pomme de terre n'est pas un fruit—c'est un légume.**
8. **Plus de céréales, s'il vous plaît.**
9. **Le chat mange notre salade de poulet !**
10. **Mon papa adore boire du café, mais je n'aime pas le café.**

Answers on page 277.

EXPRESSIONS FRANÇAISES

N'est-ce pas ? is a very common French expression. Regardless of how it looks in French, the pronunciation only has two syllables, sounding something like *ness pah*. People use this expression all the time in France—and even English speakers can use it to give a question a sophisticated flavor.

N'est-ce pas ? translates literally as *isn't it?* It can translate to many different sentences, depending on the question being asked.

In addition to being a cool French expression, **n'est-ce pas ?** is also another way of asking *yes/no* questions.

Est-ce que tu parles français ? (*Do you speak French?*)

Tu parles français, n'est-ce pas ? (*You speak French, don't you?*)

GENERAL ADVICE

Congratulations! You made it all the way to the end of the book!

In closing, the authors would like to offer a few thoughts which you may find helpful. This book was designed to cover the beginning stages of French grammar in the easiest way possible. But, there is still a lot you do not know. So, here are a few thoughts and suggestions to help you continue your study of French.

First, we recommend that you take a closer look at the French verb system. In this book, we have tried to help you build a good foundation of knowledge about French verbs, but there is still much more to learn. For example, you still need to learn about the various French verb tenses, such as the past tenses and the future tense.

Also, in this book, in order to make memorization easier, we have only made use of a small number of words. So, you should constantly strive to increase your French vocabulary. One way to do that is to use French in real-life situations. It may be difficult for you to find opportunities to speak French, but fortunately, the internet has made it easier to get in contact with other people who share your same interests. Check our website for some helpful links to get you started.

Lastly, we would like to encourage you to always be aware of your pronunciation so that you can cultivate the most authentic French pronunciation possible. One way to do this is to take advantage of the many videos on YouTube which explain and demonstrate French pronunciation. Look for links to some of these on our website.

Please take a moment to reflect on all you have learned. Although you have come a long way from lesson one, there is still much to learn. We, the authors, sincerely hope that this book has been enjoyable and profitable for you. We also hope that the knowledge you have gained from this book will become the foundation of a lifetime of enjoyment of the French language.

ANSWER KEY

LESSON SEVEN

1. *Boy*
2. *A boy*

LESSON NINE

1. *Girl*
2. *A girl*
3. *Boy*
4. *A boy*

LESSON TEN

1. *Girl and boy*
2. *Boy and girl*
3. *A girl and a boy*
4. *A boy and a girl*
5. *A girl*
6. *A boy*

LESSON ELEVEN

1. *The boy*
2. *A boy*
3. *A girl*
4. *A girl and a boy*
5. *A boy and a girl*
6. *The boy and a girl*
7. *A girl and the boy*

LESSON 12

1. *Brother*
2. *The brother*
3. *A brother*
4. *The boy and a girl*
5. *A girl*
6. *A girl and a boy*
7. *A boy*
8. *A girl and the boy*

LESSON 13

1. *The girl*
2. *The girl and the boy*
3. *The boy and the girl*
4. *The boy*
5. *A girl and a boy*
6. *A boy and a girl*
7. *The brother*
8. *A boy*
9. *A girl*
10. *A brother*

LESSON 15

1. *The sister*
2. *A sister*
3. *A sister and a brother*
4. *A girl*
5. *The boy*
6. *A brother and a sister*
7. *The sister and the brother*
8. *The girl*
9. *The brother and the sister*
10. *A girl and a boy*

LESSON 17

1. An
2. A
3. A
4. An
5. A

LESSON 20

1. **l'enfant**
2. **l'orange**
3. **l'arbre**
4. **l'ordinateur**
5. **l'image**

LESSON 22

1. Sort of silent, nasalizing the vowel (because **garçon** starts with a consonant)
2. Fully pronounced *n* sound (because **arbre** starts with a vowel)
3. Sort of silent, nasalizing the vowel (because **frère** starts with a consonant)
4. Fully pronounced *n* sound (because **ami** starts with a vowel)
5. Fully pronounced *n* sound (because **enfant** starts with a vowel)

LESSON 24

1. *My brother*
2. *My (male) friend*
3. *My sister*
4. *My brother and my sister*
5. *A (male) friend and my sister*
6. *The girl and the boy*
7. *The (male) friend*
8. *A (male) friend*
9. *A (female) friend*
10. *A (female) friend and a (male) friend*

LESSON 25

1. *My (male) friend*
2. *My (female) friend*
3. *My sister*
4. *My sister and my (male) friend*
5. *The boy and the girl*
6. *A girl and my sister*
7. *My brother and my (female) friend*
8. *The (male) friend and the (female) friend*
9. *A (male) friend and my brother*
10. *My (female) friend and my sister*

LESSON 26

1. *My son*
2. *My daughter*
3. *A girl*
4. *My daughter and my son*
5. *My son and a boy*
6. *My sister and my daughter*
7. *My (female) friend and my sister*
8. *The (male) friend and the boy*
9. *My brother and my (male) friend*
10. *My sister and a girl*

LESSON 27

1. *Your (male) friend*
2. *Your sister*
3. *Your (female) friend*
4. *Your brother and your sister*
5. *Your daughter and my daughter*
6. *A (male) friend and a (female) friend*
7. *Your daughter and my son*
8. *The boy and my (female) friend*
9. *The (female) friend*
10. *A girl and a boy*

LESSON 28

1. Plural
2. Singular
3. Singular
4. Singular
5. Plural
6. Singular
7. Plural
8. Plural
9. Plural
10. Singular

LESSON 29

1. **garçons**
2. **amis**
3. **sœurs**
4. **amies**
5. **frères**
6. **filles**
7. **fils**

LESSON 31

1. *The boys*
2. *The friends* (could be male only or a mixed group)
3. *The sons*
4. *The sisters*
5. *Your (male) friend*
6. *Your (female) friend and my brother*
7. *My daughter and your sister*
8. *The boy and the girl*
9. *A (female) friend*
10. *The (female) friend*

LESSON 32

1. *A man*
2. *The man*
3. *The men*
4. *My son and my sister*
5. *Your brother and my daughter*
6. *The (female) friends*
7. *The friends* (could be male only or a mixed group)
8. *My (female) friend*
9. *The (female) friend*
10. *The boys and the girls*

LESSON 33

1. *The woman*
2. *My wife*
3. *My wife and the man*
4. *The women and the men*
5. *My husband and my daughter*
6. *The man and my (male) friend*
7. *Your son and my daughter*
8. *The sisters and a brother*
9. *The (female) friends*
10. *A girl*

LESSON 34

1. *My sons*
2. *Your daughters*
3. *Your friends* (could be male only or a mixed group)
4. *Your sisters and my brothers*
5. *My husband and your friends* (could be male only or a mixed group)
6. *The man and your sister*
7. *Your wife and my daughter*
8. *The (male) friend*
9. *The brothers and the (female) friends*
10. *A girl and a boy*

LESSON 35

1. *The parents*
2. *My parents and your parents*
3. *Your daughters and a boy*
4. *Your son and your husband*
5. *The women and the man*
6. *The friends* (could be male only or a mixed group)
7. *My wife*
8. *Your sister and your (female) friends*
9. *My daughters and your brother*
10. *The (male) friend*

LESSON 36

1. *The children*
2. *My children*
3. *My daughter and your friends*
4. *My parents and my husband*
5. *Your sisters and the children*
6. *My son and the boys*
7. *The child and the woman*
8. *Your wife and your sisters*
9. *A man and a woman*
10. *My wife and my brother*

LESSON 37

1. *A man*
2. *Some men*
3. *A woman*
4. *Some women*
5. *My brother and my sister*
6. *The man and the woman*
7. *The sisters and the brothers*
8. *Your friends and some girls*
9. *The friend and my daughter*
10. *My husband, my sons, and some boys*

LESSON 39

1. *Good day, my friend.*
2. *Goodbye, my son.*
3. *My sisters and some girls.*
4. *Some friends and my brother.*
5. *The friend.*
6. *Good night, my brother.*
7. *The man and the woman.*
8. *Your sister and the girls.*
9. *Good evening, my brother.*
10. *Your daughters.*

LESSON 40

1. *My father.*
2. *Your mother.*
3. *Your father and your mother.*
4. *Good day, Dad.*
5. *Goodbye, Mom.*
6. *The men and the boys.*
7. *My sisters and your daughter.*
8. *A friend and my mother.*
9. *The man and your brothers.*
10. *Some boys and my sons.*

LESSON 41

1. Kate (subject) walks (verb)
2. car (subject) is (verb)
3. sister (subject) likes (verb)
4. horse (subject) is (verb)
5. Harry (subject) told (verb)
6. Bob (subject) plays (verb)
7. Mark (subject) plays (verb)
8. brother (subject) cleans (verb)
9. Julia (subject) loves (verb)
10. students (subject) finished (verb)

LESSON 42

1. he (takes the place of *Alfred*)
2. it (takes the place of *locker room*)
3. she
4. they (takes the place of *kids*)
5. he (takes the place of *Johnny*)
6. we
7. they
8. you
9. it (takes the place of *rabbit*)
10. they (takes the place of *children*)

LESSON 43

1. *I am your father.*
2. *I am your sister.*
3. *I am a man.*
4. *I am your husband.*
5. *The children and the parents.*
6. *Good day, my daughter.*
7. *My wife and some children.*
8. *Goodbye, children.*
9. *My children, my wife, and my mother.*
10. *The friend.*

LESSON 44

1. *I am.*
2. *I am not.*
3. *I am not a child.*
4. *Goodbye, my friend.*
5. *Some boys and some girls.*
6. *The friend, the mother, and the father.*
7. *Good day, my children.*
8. *My parents and a sister.*
9. *The women and the men.*
10. *The child and your friends.*

LESSON 45

1. *You are my friend.*
2. *You are not my friend.*
3. *I am your brother.*
4. *I am not a man.*
5. *The children and the parents.*
6. *I am your mother.*
7. *Good day, my sons.*
8. *A boy and some girls.*
9. *Goodbye, my friend.*
10. *I am your daughter; I am not your son.*

LESSON 46

1. *The man is my father.*
2. *The woman is my mother.*
3. *My sister is not your friend.*
4. *My son is your friend.*
5. *The child is not my brother.*
6. *You are my friend.*
7. *I am not a woman.*
8. *My wife and the children.*
9. *Good evening, my friends.*
10. *Your sisters and some girls.*

LESSON 47

1. *He is not my brother.*
2. *She is my sister.*
3. *He is my friend.*
4. *She is my mother.*
5. *I am your father.*
6. *You are not my brother.*
7. *A man, a woman, and some children.*
8. *Your parents and my friends.*
9. *My daughter and a friend.*
10. *Goodbye, my friend.*

LESSON 48

1. *Good day, sir.*
2. *Good day, Mr. Smith.*
3. *Mr. Smith is my husband.*
4. *He is my father.*
5. *Mrs. Jones is not my sister.*
6. *Goodbye, miss.*
7. *She is the girl.*
8. *You are my wife.*
9. *I am a girl.*
10. *My parents and your children.*

LESSON 49

1. *We are your parents.*
2. *Mr. Jones is my brother.*
3. *He is Mr. Smith.*
4. *Good day, ma'am.*
5. *She is not Mrs. Smith; she is Mrs. Jones.*
6. *You are my brother.*
7. *I am not your son.*
8. *The women and some children.*
9. *The friend.*
10. *Some friends and my sisters.*

LESSON 50

1. *Y'all are my friends.*
2. *Y'all are my children.*
3. *You are Mrs. Smith.*
4. *Good night, my friend.*
5. *He is my dad.*
6. *Mr. Smith is my father.*
7. *Goodbye, Mrs. Jones.*
8. *We are not your daughters.*
9. *You are not my brother.*
10. *She is my friend.*

LESSON 52

1. *They are my sisters.*
2. *They are your friends.*
3. *They are not my daughters.*
4. *Y'all are my friends.*
5. *We are your friends.*
6. *Good day, Mr. Jones.*
7. *She is my mother.*
8. *You are a boy.*
9. *I am not a child.*
10. *The men and some women.*

LESSON 54

1. I (subject) first person, singular
2. You (subject) second person, singular
3. She (subject) third person, singular
4. We (subject) first person, plural
5. Y'all (subject) second person, plural
6. They (subject) third person, plural
7. He (subject) third person, singular
8. It (subject) third person, singular
9. Y'all (subject) second person, plural
10. flowers (subject) third person, plural

LESSON 56

1. *My son and some dogs.*
2. *The dog is my friend.*
3. *The dogs are my friends.*
4. *Mr. Smith is not my father.*
5. *They are my sisters.*
6. *Y'all are my sisters.*
7. *We are not your friends—we are your parents.*
8. *Your sister is my friend.*
9. *Mr. and Mrs. Jones are my parents.*
10. *You are my friend.*

LESSON 57

1. *A man* OR *one man.*
2. *A sister* OR *one sister.*
3. *356-0142 (three five six zero one four two).*
4. *Two boys and five women.*
5. *The girl, some boys, and six dogs.*
6. *They are my daughters.*
7. *We are not your parents.*
8. *Y'all are my brothers.*
9. *He is my father.*
10. *I am your child.*

LESSON 58

1. *Seven friends.*
2. *Nine children.*
3. *790-8415 (seven nine zero eight four one five)*
4. *Ten dogs and twelve children.*
5. *Eleven girls and some boys.*
6. *I am your sister and y'all are my brothers.*
7. *You are my friend.*
8. *Mrs. Smith is not my sister.*
9. *They are not my children.*
10. *We are the parents and they are the children.*

LESSON 59

1. *Two cats and four dogs.*
2. *Three brothers and five sisters.*
3. *Six cats and nine dogs.*
4. *Seven boys and ten girls.*
5. *My cat is my friend.*
6. *My cats are my friends.*
7. *You are my friend.*
8. *We are not sisters.*
9. *Y'all are my friends.*
10. *She is my friend.*

LESSON 60

1. *I have three dogs.*
2. *I have two cats.*
3. *I have eight cats and ten dogs.*
4. *I have some dogs.*
5. *Your sister is my sister.*
6. *They are my friends.*
7. *I have a son and nine daughters.*
8. *I am your mother.*
9. *Y'all are my friends.*
10. *Mr. Smith is my friend.*

LESSON 62

1. *I have ten dogs and also a cat.*
2. *I have four brothers. I also have three sisters.*
3. *I have twelve cats. I also have some dogs.*
4. *My dog is my friend.*
5. *Good day, ma'am—I am Mr. Jones.*
6. *I have a sister.*
7. *She is my mother.*
8. *We are your parents.*
9. *I am a woman and you are a man.*
10. *You are Mrs. Smith.*

LESSON 63

1. *I have the books.*
2. *I do not have five books.*
3. *I have seven cats and also nine dogs.*
4. *I have some cats. I also have a dog.*
5. *My cat is my friend.*
6. *They are my brothers.*
7. *My daughter is your friend.*
8. *You are Mrs. Jones.*
9. *I am your sister.*
10. *I am the man.*

LESSON 64

1. *I do not have three cars.*
2. *I have some books.*
3. *I have four cars.*
4. *I have eight cats. I also have two dogs.*
5. *I have a car.*
6. *I am a man.*
7. *You are not my dog—you are my cat.*
8. *The girls are my friends.*
9. *I have three books.*
10. *I have a sister.*

LESSON 66

1. *I have some rice.*
2. *I have some turkey.*
3. *I have some money.*
4. *I am a cat.*
5. *I have some cats. I also have a dog.*
6. *I have some books.*
7. *I have three cars.*
8. *Your sisters are my friends.*
9. *They have some dogs.*
10. *Y'all are my parents.*

LESSON 67

1. *I have some food.*
2. *I have some money.*
3. *I have some turkey.*
4. *I have some rice.*
5. *I have two cars.*
6. *I have five books.*
7. *I have some brothers and also some sisters.*
8. *We are sisters.*
9. *You are my friend.*
10. *She is my wife.*

LESSON 68

1. *I have a dollar.*
2. *I have ten euros and nine francs.*
3. *I have four francs and also a euro.* OR *I have four francs and also one euro.*
4. *I have some money… I have five euros and eleven dollars.*
5. *I have seven cats. I also have eight dogs.*
6. *I have some turkey and some rice.*
7. *You are Mr. Jones.*
8. *I do not have my book.*
9. *I have my car.*
10. *I am not a child.*

LESSON 69

1. *You have five euros.*
2. *You have some money.*
3. *You have some rice and I have some turkey.*
4. *I do not have your money.*
5. *You are not a mother.*
6. *You have two cats.*
7. *You have eight euros and three dollars.*
8. *He is not my father.*
9. *You have some food.*
10. *You are my friend… we are friends.*

LESSON 70

1. *He has my money.*
2. *She has some books.*
3. *My son has some money.*
4. *He does not have three dollars.*
5. *He has nine children—two sons and also seven daughters.*
6. *I am your friend.*
7. *You have ten sisters and also a brother.*
8. *My daughter has my car.*
9. *They are my friends, and y'all are my brothers.*
10. *You have some turkey and some rice.*

LESSON 71

1. *I have a dog, but you have a cat.*
2. *You do not have your cat, but you have your dog.*
3. *My cat is my friend, but your dog is your friend.*
4. *My brother has my money.*
5. *I have four dogs. I also have five cats.*
6. *Mrs. Smith has my books.*
7. *We are friends, but they are not my friends.*
8. *She has some food.*
9. *You do not have six euros.*
10. *I have some rice.*

LESSON 72

1. *We have some friends.*
2. *We do not have three sisters.*
3. *You have a dollar. I also have a dollar.* OR *You have one dollar. I also have one dollar.*
4. *She does not have my car.*
5. *I do not have your money.*
6. *The girls are my sisters and the boys are my brothers.*
7. *She has five sons and also six daughters.*
8. *We have some turkey.*
9. *My father has the car.*
10. *You are my friend, but he is my brother.*

LESSON 73

1. *Y'all have my books.* (OR, using formal speech) *You have my books.*
2. *Y'all have some rice.* (OR, using formal speech) *You have some rice.*
3. *We have my car.*
4. *He has some money.*
5. *You do not have ten euros.*
6. *You have seven sisters, but I have twelve sisters and a brother.*
7. *My sister has my car.*
8. *They are my children.*
9. *The children are your brothers and your sisters.*
10. *She is not my friend.*

LESSON 74

1. *They have my money!*
2. *They do not have three cars—they have two cars.*
3. *They have three children, but we have two children.*
4. *Mrs. Jones, you are not my mother.*
5. *I have four cats and also some dogs.*
6. *The boys are my sons.*
7. *Y'all have some money.* (OR, using formal speech) *You have some money.*
8. *Mr. Smith has six brothers.*
9. *You have some friends.*
10. *She has ten euros.*

LESSON 76

1. *I have some rice.*
2. *I do not have any rice.*
3. *You have some money.*
4. *You do not have any money.*
5. *We do not have any children.*
6. *Y'all have eight children, but they do not have any children.* (OR, using formal speech) *You have eight children, but they do not have any children.*
7. *I do not have a car.*
8. *I do not have the car.*
9. *My sister has ten euros. She also has five dollars.*
10. *We do not have any food.*

LESSON 77

1. *My sister has her dog.*
2. *My brother has his cats.*
3. *She has her money.*
4. *Mr. Jones has his car.*
5. *They have nine dollars.*
6. *Y'all do not have five dollars.* (OR, using formal speech) *You do not have five dollars.*
7. *I have ten euros, but my friend does not have any money.*
8. *We have a dog, but we do not have a cat.*
9. *They have some food.*
10. *The children have some books.*

LESSON 78

1. *They have our dog!*
2. *He has y'all's book.* (OR, using formal speech) *He has your book.*
3. *We have their car.*
4. *The dog has our food!*
5. *We have their books.*
6. *You have our books.*
7. *My brother has y'all's cats.* (OR, using formal speech) *My brother has your cats.*
8. *They have eight dollars, but we do not have any money.*
9. *Mr. Smith has four cats and also a dog.*
10. *He has his car, but I do not have a car.*

LESSON 80

1. *My brother's money.*
2. *The woman's car.*
3. *My mother's food.*
4. *I have my sister's dog.*
5. *My brother's friend does not have his car.*
6. *Andre's brother has ten euros.*
7. *We do not have a dog, but we have a cat.*
8. *You have our book.*
9. *Y'all have our books.* (OR, using formal speech) *You have our books.*
10. *They have y'all's books.* (OR, using formal speech) *They have your books.*

LESSON 81

1. *The man's car.*
2. *The boy's cat.*
3. *The girl's money.*
4. *I have my brother's car.*
5. *Your son has his car.*
6. *His/her parents have seven children, but we do not have any children.*
7. *They do not have any food.*
8. *I have some rice, but you do not have any rice.*
9. *I do not have a book.*
10. *She does not have the book.*

LESSON 83

1. *I am hungry.*
2. *I am not hungry.*
3. *The boy's dog is not thirsty.*
4. *Our cats are thirsty.*
5. *You do not have their car.*
6. *My daughter has my brother's car.*
7. *My dog is hungry, but he does not have any food.*
8. *Y'all have our books.* (OR, using formal speech) *You have our books.*
9. *We have some food, but y'all are not hungry.* (OR, using formal speech) *We have some food, but you are not hungry.*
10. *You have our dog and also his/her dog.*

LESSON 84

1. *I want some money.*
2. *You want the man's car, but I do not want the car.*
3. *He wants ten dollars, but we do not have any money.*
4. *We do not want a cat.*
5. *My dog is hungry, but he does not have any food.*
6. *My brother does not have a dog, but his son wants a dog.*
7. *I am thirsty, but y'all are not thirsty.* (OR, using formal speech) *I am thirsty but you are not thirsty.*
8. *Our children want our money and also our car.*
9. *My sister has our dogs, and we have her dogs.*
10. *He has y'all's dogs and also their dogs.* (OR, using formal speech) *He has your dogs and also their dogs.*

LESSON 85

1. *You want some food because you are hungry.*
2. *He does not have a car because he does not have any money.*
3. *We are hungry, but they do not have any food.*
4. *My husband wants a daughter and a son also.*
5. *The children want seven dollars.*
6. *Y'all have a dog, but y'all want a cat.* (OR, using formal speech) *You have a dog, but you want a cat.*
7. *I want my father's car because I do not have a car.*
8. *She wants some food because she is hungry.*
9. *Their cats are thirsty because they do not have any water.*
10. *Y'all's dog has our turkey!* (OR, using formal speech) *Your dog has our turkey!*

LESSON 86

1. *I want some water because I am thirsty.*
2. *They want some water because they are thirsty.*
3. *My father is hungry and he wants some food.*
4. *We are hungry, but we do not have any money.*
5. *She wants her father's car.*
6. *Y'all want our cats.* (OR, using formal speech) *You want our cats.*
7. *You want some turkey because you are hungry.*
8. *I want their car.*
9. *My brother has his money—twelve euros, eight dollars, and also three francs.*
10. *I have eleven cats, but I do not have any friends.*

LESSON 87

1. *I speak English.*
2. *Y'all speak French.* (OR, using formal speech) *You speak French.*
3. *My parents speak English.*
4. *We speak French and also English.*
5. *We want some rice, but they want some turkey.*
6. *He does not speak French.*
7. *We are thirsty because we do not have any water.*
8. *The woman's cat is hungry—he wants some food.*
9. *The children are hungry and thirsty—they want some water.*
10. *They want our food because they do not have their food.*

LESSON 89

1. *I speak English every day.*
2. *My cat wants our food every day.*
3. *Every day, you speak French.*
4. *She has a cat and four dogs, and her dogs are hungry.*
5. *We have twelve euros, but we do not have any francs.*
6. *Y'all's sister is my friend.* (OR, using formal speech) *Your sister is my friend.*
7. *They speak French every day, but we speak English.*
8. *My dog wants some food every day.*
9. *We want some water because we are thirsty.*
10. *My dad's friends are hungry, but we do not have any food.*

LESSON 91

> **mundus** becomes **monde**
> **pānis** becomes **pain**
> **saeculum** becomes **siècle**
> **amīcus** becomes **ami**
> **liber** becomes **livre**
> **ecclēsia** becomes **église**
> **tempus** becomes **temps**
> **cor** becomes **cœur**
> **corpus** becomes **corps**
> **pax** becomes **paix**
> **mors, mortis** becomes **mort**

LESSON 92

1. *Every day I buy food.*
2. *We buy food every day.*
3. *The men do not buy food every day.*
4. *My sister's cat is hungry, but my sister does not have any food.*
5. *I do not have any food and I do not have any money.*
6. *You speak English, but I speak French.*
7. *My father does not have his car—he has his brother's car.*
8. *My sister does not speak English, but she speaks French.*
9. *We speak French every day, but they do not speak English.*
10. *I am not buying the car!*

LESSON 93

1. *Do we have our car?*
2. *Do they buy food every day?*
3. *Do you have a cat?*
4. *Do y'all have three dogs?* (OR, using formal speech) *Do you have three dogs?*
5. *Do you want your father's car?*
6. *Is she your friend?*
7. *Do we have any rice?*
8. *Does the cat have y'all's food?* (OR, using formal speech) *Does the cat have your food?*
9. *His/her dog has some food, but he is not hungry.*
10. *My father's brother is hungry because he does not have any food.*

LESSON 94

1. *Do you buy food every day?*
2. *No, I do not buy food every day.*
3. *Does y'all's brother have a child?* (OR, using formal speech) *Does your brother have a child?*
4. *Yes, our brother has three sons. He also has a daughter.*
5. *Are the men hungry?*
6. *Yes, the men are hungry, but we do not have any food.*
7. *Are you a mother?*
8. *No, I am not a mother because I do not have any children.*
9. *Do you speak French?*
10. *No, I speak English, but my sisters speak French every day.*

LESSON 95

1. *I eat food every day.*
2. *The boys eat food every day.*
3. *We eat every day.*
4. *Is Mrs. Jones hungry?*
5. *No, Mrs. Jones is not hungry, but I am hungry.*
6. *They buy food every day.*
7. *My sister's children want some water because they are thirsty.*
8. *The cat is eating our turkey!*
9. *We speak French, but y'all do not speak French.* (OR, using formal speech) *We speak French, but you do not speak French.*
10. *She is not buying a car because her husband does not have any money.*

LESSON 96

1. *We always speak French.*
2. *They always eat turkey.*
3. *You buy food every day.*
4. *Does your brother have the car?*
5. *Yes, my brother has the car.*
6. *No, my brother does not have the car.*
7. *I eat rice every day.*
8. *My daughter's cat wants some water because he is thirsty.*
9. *Y'all's sons do not have their books.* (OR, using formal speech) *Your sons do not have their books.*
10. *Y'all's children are hungry, and they are thirsty also.* (OR, using formal speech) *Your children are hungry and they are thirsty also.*

LESSON 97

1. *I always drink water.*
2. *She is thirsty, but she does not want water.*
3. *Their brothers speak French every day.*
4. *Do you drink water every day?*
5. *Yes, we drink water every day.*
6. *She is eating food because she is hungry.*
7. *My parents buy food every day.*
8. *My dogs eat food and drink water every day.*
9. *My dad has four dogs, but he does not have a cat.*
10. *She wants her father's money because she wants a car.*

LESSON 98

1. *Y'all buy food every week.* (OR, using formal speech) *You buy food every week.*
2. *Our mother buys food every week.*
3. *Your parents buy food every week.*
4. *My mother's dog is hungry because he does not have any food.*
5. *We want some food and some money.*
6. *My cats always want my food.*
7. *Andre's daughter speaks English and also French.*
8. *The men are my brothers and the women are my sisters.*
9. *Do y'all want a car?* (OR, using formal speech) *Do you want a car?*
10. *No, I do not want a car.*

LESSON 99

1. *I work every day.*
2. *Our sisters work every day.*
3. *We buy food every week.*
4. *Does your brother's friend work every day?*
5. *Yes, she works every day.*
6. *We drink water every day.*
7. *They do not speak English, but they speak French.*
8. *We are thirsty because we do not have any water.*
9. *My friends always have money because they work every day.*
10. *My dog is drinking his water, and he also wants his food.*

LESSON 101

1. Preposition: behind
   Object of the preposition: couch
2. Preposition: beside
   Object of the preposition: lamp
3. Preposition: in
   Object of the preposition: trunk
4. Preposition: through
   Object of the preposition: tunnel
5. Preposition: under
   Object of the preposition: house
6. Preposition: before
   Object of the preposition: lunch
7. Preposition: after
   Object of the preposition: school
8. Preposition: by
   Object of the preposition: post office
9. Preposition: on
   Object of the preposition: campus
10. Preposition: beyond
    Object of the preposition: mountain

LESSON 102

1. *My mother goes to the bank every week.*
2. *We go to the store every week.*
3. *Do your parents go to the store every day?*
4. *No, they go to the store every week.*
5. *I am going to the bank because I do not have any money.*
6. *The boys and the girls work every day.*
7. *You drink water every day because you are always thirsty.*
8. *I want Andre's car, but I do not have any money.*
9. *We are not buying a car because we do not have any money.*
10. *My mother's friend speaks English. She also speaks French.*

LESSON 103

1. *We go to the mall every week.*
2. *My friends go to the mall every day.*
3. *My daughter goes to the mall every week.*
4. *Do you go to the bank every week?*
5. *Yes, I go to the bank every week.*
6. *My children want a cat.*
7. *We go to the mall every week because we are friends.*
8. *We are not eating rice because we do not have any rice.*
9. *Their children always work, but our children do not work.* OR *Their children are always working, but our children are not working.*
10. *My sister has a cat, and her cat wants water because he is thirsty.*

LESSON 104

1. *I am going to the store.*
2. *I am at the store.*
3. *My father is going to the bank.*
4. *My mother works at the bank every day.*
5. *Our father is at the store.*
6. *Some friends are going to the mall.*
7. *Do y'all drink water every day?* (OR, using formal speech) *Do you drink water every day?*
8. *Yes, I drink water every day because I am always thirsty.*
9. *My brother and his children are going to the mall.*
10. *My cat is eating his food.*

LESSON 105

1. *I am at the park.*
2. *They go to the store every week.*
3. *Do you go to the park every day?*
4. *No, but I go to the park every week.*
5. *We always speak French, but my parents do not speak French.*
6. *We are not going to the mall because our parents do not have any money.*
7. *My sister's friend works at the bank.* OR *My sister's friend is working at the bank.*
8. *He always drinks water.*
9. *I want a car, but we are not buying a car.*
10. *We eat at the mall every week.*

LESSON 106

1. *I am going to the park with my friends.*
2. *I eat with my sisters at the mall every week.*
3. *He works with my brother every day at my father's store.*
4. *I speak English with my friends, but I always speak French with my parents.*
5. *I drink water every day.*
6. *Y'all speak French every day.* (OR, using formal speech) *You speak French every day.*
7. *My children do not speak English, but they speak French.*
8. *Do we have any food?*
9. *We do not have any money, but my father's friend has two dollars.*
10. *My mother is going to the bank because she wants some money.*

LESSON 107

1. *The girls go to the mall with me every week.*
2. *Does he eat with you every week?*
3. *I go to the park with them every day.*
4. *We go to the park with him every week.*
5. *The girls want water because they are thirsty.*
6. *Your dog wants water, but our dog is not thirsty.*
7. *My brother works with me every day.*
8. *My mother's friend speaks French, but I speak English.*
9. *Mr. Smith works at the store every day with his children.*
10. *Our dogs always drink water.*

LESSON 108

1. *Are you going to the beach?*
2. *My friends go to the beach with me every week.*
3. *We are at the beach with our dog.*
4. *He goes to the beach with his parents every week.*
5. *They always go to the beach, but we always go to the park.*
6. *She goes to the beach with him every week.*
7. *They are at the beach with their friends.*
8. *I want my sister's car because I do not have a car.*
9. *He is not going to the store with you.*
10. *I buy food every day at the store.*

LESSON 109

1. *You often go to the park with him, but you do not go to the park with me.*
2. *You do not often go to the store, but I go to the store every day.*
3. *They are going to the beach with their parents.*
4. *My daughter works at the store with her friends.* OR *My daughter is working at the store with her friends.*
5. *Do your sisters often go to the mall with you?*
6. *Yes, I eat with my sisters at the mall every week.*
7. *We often drink water because we are thirsty.*
8. *We have y'all's books.* (OR, using formal speech) *We have your books.*
9. *She is buying food at the store because we do not have any food.*
10. *You often go to the mall with their friends and them, but you do not often go to the mall with our friends.*

LESSON 110

1. *I go to school every day.*
2. *We go to school with our friends every day.*
3. *My dog often goes to school with me.*
4. *He is going to the store because his cat does not have any food.*
5. *She goes to the beach with him every week.*
6. *The children are at school with their friends.*
7. *Y'all's dog always goes to school with the children.* (OR, using formal speech) *Your dog always goes to school with the children.*
8. *The cats drink water and eat food every day.*
9. *The cat is eating my book!*
10. *My brother speaks French and English because he works at the bank.*

LESSON 111

1. *I often see the car.*
2. *We see our mother at the park every day.*
3. *Y'all go to the store every day because y'all buy food every day.* (OR, using formal speech) *You go to the store every day because you buy food every day.*
4. *The children see their friends at school every day.*
5. *Y'all see my brother at the mall every week.* (OR, using formal speech) *You see my brother at the mall every week.*
6. *You work with us every day.*
7. *We always go to the beach with them.*
8. *I am not going to the store with you because I do not want food.*
9. *Does your father go to the bank every day?*
10. *Yes, because my father works at the bank.*

LESSON 112

1. newspaper
2. movie
3. trombone
4. baseball
5. fish
6. radio
7. building
8. speech
9. wallet
10. deer

LESSON 114

1. *You see me.*
2. *I see you.*
3. *He does not see her.*
4. *She sees him.*
5. *They see us.*
6. *We see y'all.* (OR, using formal speech) *We see you.*
7. *We do not see them.*
8. *I often see them.*
9. *We often see her.*
10. *I do not often see y'all.* (OR, using formal speech) *I do not often see you.*

LESSON 115

1. *I never go to the store, but my parents go to the store every week.*
2. *Do you go to the beach often?*
3. *No, I never go to the beach.*
4. *We often go to the mall, but we never have any money.*
5. *We go to school every day.*
6. *I never see them at the park.*
7. *They often see you with your friends at the beach.*
8. *My friends do not have any money, but I have five dollars.*
9. *He never goes to the park with his cats.*
10. *We go to the beach with them every week.*

LESSON 116

1. *They never go to the mall without money.*
2. *We never go to the park without water.*
3. *She never goes to the mall without you.*
4. *The women always speak French.*
5. *My brother and his friends always go with me to the beach.*
6. *I see you with your friends every day.*
7. *Our children never go to school without their books.*
8. *Your cat sees me, but he does not see my dog.*
9. *Do you often see my mother's friend?*
10. *Yes, I see her with her friends every week.*

LESSON 117

1. *I go to work every day.*
2. *I want a job.*
3. *My father goes to work every day.*
4. *My son wants a job because he wants a car.*
5. *My sister has some dogs, but she does not have a cat.*
6. *I see you often because we eat with you every week.*
7. *Does your brother have a job?*
8. *Yes, he always has money because he works at the bank.*
9. *She never goes to the beach without her dogs.*
10. *She always goes to the mall with me.*

LESSON 119

1. *My family is at the beach.*
2. *My brother goes to the park with his family every week.*
3. *My family eats with me every day.*
4. *I have a job and a car.*
5. *She goes to work every day.*
6. *My family never goes to the park without our dogs.*
7. *Are you at the store with the children?*
8. *They see me at the bank every week.*
9. *We often see them with their children at the park.*
10. *You go to the mall with them every week.*

LESSON 120

1. to wash
2. to play
3. There is no infinitive in this sentence.
4. to be
5. to forgive
6. to return
7. to play
8. There is no infinitive in this sentence.
9. to buy
10. There is no infinitive in this sentence.

LESSON 121

1. *I want to speak French with my friends at school.*
2. *They want to speak English.*
3. *We do not want to speak French with you.*
4. *She wants to speak English with her brother.*
5. *He does not want to speak English—he wants to speak French.*
6. *My family never goes to the beach without water.*
7. *My friends see me at the mall every week.*
8. *I am going to the beach with them.*
9. *Do you want to speak French with me?*
10. *I am at the store because I am buying food.*

LESSON 124

1. *I want to buy clothes.*
2. *We are buying clothes at the store.*
3. *They want to have a cat, but their father does not want to have a cat.*
4. *Does your sister have a job?*
5. *No, but my sister wants to work at the bank.*
6. *Mr. Jones' family often goes to the beach.*
7. *I want to go to the store, but I do not have my car.*
8. *I want to drink water because I am thirsty.*
9. *We never go to the beach without you.*
10. *I want to see my friends at the mall.*

LESSON 125

1. *I want to buy clothes today.*
2. *We do not want to eat turkey today.*
3. *You want to go to the beach today with the children.*
4. *My friends want to go to the mall today, but they do not have a car.*
5. *They want to buy clothes today, but they do not have any money.*
6. *Do y'all often go to the mall with y'all's family?* (OR, using formal speech) *Do you often go to the mall with your family?*
7. *No, we never go to the mall.*
8. *Our dog wants to be at the beach.*
9. *My friends see me at school every day.*
10. *My sister wants to buy a car because her son wants a car.*

LESSON 126

1. *My family needs a car.*
2. *I need to drink water because I am thirsty.*
3. *My dad needs to buy food.*
4. *They need to go to the store because they need to buy clothes.*
5. *We want to go to the beach today.*
6. *My parents want to have a dog.*
7. *The girl wants to go to the mall with her friends.*
8. *The children want to eat at the mall, but we are not hungry.*
9. *Y'all never want to go to the beach* (OR, using formal speech) *You never want to go to the beach.*
10. *My friends never see me without a book.*

LESSON 127

1. *I need to go to the bank tomorrow.*
2. *We want to go to the beach today.*
3. *She wants to go to the store tomorrow, but we need to buy food today.*
4. *I need to go to the mall because my daughter needs to buy clothes.*
5. *Do you have a family, Mr. Smith?*
6. *They need to eat food because they are hungry.*
7. *She wants to speak French with me, but I do not speak French.*
8. *I do not want to go to the store with them today.*
9. *My friends often see me at the store.*
10. *My men never work without food.*

LESSON 128

1. *I am able to (I can) go to the park.*
2. *I am able to (I can) speak French, but I am not able to (I cannot) speak English.*
3. *I am able to (I can) go to the park tomorrow.*
4. *I am not able to (I cannot) buy a car today.*
5. *I am not able to (I cannot) work with you every day.*
6. *We want to buy clothes today.*
7. *He does not need to buy clothes, but he wants to go to the mall.*
8. *I want to see my friends.*
9. *Do y'all have any children?* (OR, using formal speech) *Do you have any children?*
10. *We never go to the beach without our dogs.*

LESSON 129

1. *You are not able to (you cannot) go to the bank because you do not have a car.*
2. *She is able to (she can) buy a car because she works at the bank.*
3. *We are able to (we can) go to the park, but we are not able to (we cannot) go to the beach.*
4. *Are you able to (can you) go with me to the store tomorrow?*
5. *He is not able to (he cannot) buy clothes without money.*
6. *We need a dog.*
7. *I am not able to (I cannot) go to the mall today, but I am able to (I can) go to the mall tomorrow.*
8. *Do y'all want to go to the mall?* (OR, using formal speech) *Do you want to go to the mall?*
9. *Y'all see Mrs. Jones every week at the bank.* (OR, using formal speech) *You see Mrs. Jones every week at the bank.*
10. *We are not going to the beach without a car.*

LESSON 130

1. *I carry my books to school every day.*
2. *We always carry food and water to the park.*
3. *My parents always carry money.*
4. *She is not able to (she cannot) go to the beach tomorrow.*
5. *Our dog is hungry.*
6. *He is thirsty, but he does not want to drink water.*
7. *My dog does not need clothes.*
8. *I am able to (I can) work at the bank, but I am not able to (I cannot) work at the store.*
9. *We are not able to (we cannot) go to the mall with them today because I want to see my sister and her children.*
10. *Y'all's friend often sees me at the bank.* (OR, using formal speech) *Your friend often sees me at the bank.*

LESSON 131

1. *I read two books every week.*
2. *Do you want to read a book?*
3. *We do not want to read a book today.*
4. *They always read books at school.*
5. *You are able to (you can) read French, but you are not able to (you cannot) speak French.*
6. *You need to go to school tomorrow.*
7. *We carry our books to school every day.*
8. *My sons do not want to work today, but they are able to (they can) work tomorrow.*
9. *I want to buy clothes, but we do not want to go to the mall with you.*
10. *I often see you at the park with your family.*

LESSON 132

1. *I want to read the newspaper.*
2. *My parents read the newspaper every day.*
3. *I have a job—I carry the newspapers every day.*
4. *My mother reads the newspaper with my father every day.*
5. *Do y'all go to the beach with y'all's family every week? (OR, using formal speech) Do you go to the beach with your family every week?*
6. *I do not want to go to school today.*
7. *We need to drink water every day.*
8. *They are buying clothes at the mall, but we are working at school.*
9. *She is not able to (she cannot) see her friends today, but she can go to the mall tomorrow.*
10. *They want to eat turkey because they are hungry, but we do not have any turkey.*

LESSON 133

1. *He goes to church every week.*
2. *My children are going to church with me tomorrow.*
3. *Do y'all go to church every week? (OR, using formal speech) Do you go to church every week?*
4. *We are not able to (we cannot) go to church because we do not have a car.*
5. *Y'all carry the newspapers to school every day. (OR, using formal speech) You carry the newspapers to school every day.*
6. *I am not able to (I cannot) eat turkey, but I am able to (I can) eat rice.*
7. *Mr. Jones never goes to church, but we go to church every week.*
8. *Do you want to read the newspaper today?*
9. *My dog wants to go to school with me today.*
10. *They need to buy clothes because they are going to school tomorrow.*

LESSON 134

1. *I want to read books, but I am not able (I cannot) go to the library because I do not have a car.*

2. *My sister reads the newspaper every day, but I never read the newspaper.*

3. *Do you want to go to the library?*

4. *Do y'all want to go to the library?* (OR, using formal speech) *Do you want to go to the library?*

5. *No, I do not want to read books today, but I am able to (I can) go to the library with you tomorrow.*

6. *We never go to church, but we need to go to church every week.*

7. *My dogs are not able to (they cannot) read the newspaper.*

8. *He always carries a newspaper, but I always carry two newspapers.*

9. *The dog has my father's newspaper!*

10. *I am going to the library because I want to read the books and also the newspapers.*

LESSON 136

1. *My parents often go to the mall to buy clothes.*

2. *He is going to the library to read the newspapers.*

3. *She is going to the store to buy food.*

4. *I go to the mall every week to see my friends.*

5. *They go to church every week.*

6. *Y'all are not able to (y'all cannot) buy a car.* (OR, using formal speech) *You are not able to (you cannot) buy a car.*

7. *They need to go to the store to buy food.*

8. *I carry my books to school every day.*

9. *Are you going to the bank tomorrow?*

10. *No, I am going to the bank today because I need money.*

LESSON 137

1. *We go to the restaurant to eat every week.*

2. *I often go to the restaurant to eat with my friends.*

3. *Do you want to go to the restaurant to eat?*

4. *Yes! I want to eat because I am hungry!*

5. *We are not able (we cannot) go to the restaurant today because we do not have any money.*

6. *Do you want to go to the library today?*

7. *No, I am not able to (I cannot) go to the library today, but I can go to the library tomorrow.*

8. *Mr. Jones goes to church with his family every week.*

9. *My son carries the newspapers every day because he needs money.*

10. *My father is not able to (he cannot) go to work today because he does not have a car.*

LESSON 138

1. *We have lunch every day.*
2. *My friends are having lunch with me.*
3. *Do you want to have lunch with me today?*
4. *I am not able to (I cannot) have lunch with you today, but I am able to (I can) have lunch tomorrow.*
5. *You need to have lunch.*
6. *She has lunch with her parents every day.*
7. *I want to go to the restaurant with you to have lunch.*
8. *My sister is going to the library to read books.*
9. *We are not able to (we cannot) buy a car because we do not have any money.*
10. *My parents are reading the newspaper, but they need to go to church.*

LESSON 139

1. *I go to the beach every morning.*
2. *I do not want to work this morning.*
3. *My family has lunch every day.*
4. *My sister goes to school every morning.*
5. *My father reads the newspaper every morning.*
6. *Do y'all often go to the beach with y'all's family?* (OR, using formal speech) *Do you often go to the beach with your family?*
7. *No, we never go to the beach, but we often go to the park.*
8. *I drink water every morning.*
9. *My son does not want to go to school this morning.*
10. *They are not able to (they cannot) read the book because they are children.*

LESSON 140

1. *My family has breakfast every morning.*
2. *I need to have breakfast, but we do not have any food.*
3. *Do you want to have breakfast with me this morning?*
4. *Your parents never go to the restaurant to eat.*
5. *He wants to go to the restaurant to have lunch.*
6. *I want to buy a car, but I do not have any money.*
7. *I carry my lunch with me to school every day.*
8. *We are going to the library tomorrow to read books.*
9. *My mother wants to go to the store to buy a newspaper.*
10. *Y'all are not able to (y'all cannot) go to the mall today because y'all do not have any money.* (OR, using formal speech) *You are not able to (you cannot) go to the mall today because you do not have any money.*

LESSON 141

1. *I want to go to the beach now.*
2. *I want to have lunch now because I am hungry!*
3. *My dogs want to eat now.*
4. *She wants to read her newspaper every day.*
5. *I want to go to the mall now to buy clothes.*
6. *Are you able to (can you) go to the mall with me?*
7. *We read our books every morning at school.*
8. *The children are hungry and they want to have breakfast now.*
9. *Are you going to the restaurant to have lunch?*
10. *No, I am going to the library now to see my friends.*

LESSON 142

1. *They go to the restaurant to eat every evening/night.*
2. *I want to go to the restaurant this evening/tonight.*
3. *We want to have lunch now because we are hungry.*
4. *Mr. Smith always carries his newspaper to the park.*
5. *Are we able to (can we) go to the mall to buy clothes this evening/tonight?*
6. *No, but you are able to (you can) go to the library to read your books.*
7. *He never goes to school without his books.*
8. *We see our friends at church every week.*
9. *Do you want to go to the beach this morning?*
10. *The dog is eating our breakfast!*

LESSON 143

1. *The cat is eating your dinner!*
2. *I have dinner with my family every evening/night.*
3. *They go to the restaurant to have dinner every evening/night.*
4. *My sister has dinner with me every week.*
5. *We have lunch at school every day.*
6. *She wants to have breakfast with her friends every morning.*
7. *Do you want to go to the library to read books?*
8. *No, I am not able to (I cannot) go to the library because I need to go to the beach with my friends.*
9. *You are not able to (you cannot) have breakfast this evening/tonight, but you are able to (you can) have dinner.*
10. *Today we are having breakfast at church.*

LESSON 144

1. *Your lunch is on the table.*
2. *My father's newspaper is on his desk.*
3. *The cat is on the table!*
4. *Your friends are at the beach, but you are at the library.*
5. *We do not need two desks.* OR *We do not need two offices.*
6. *I need to read the newspaper.*
7. *The children carry their books to school every day.*
8. *We are not able to (we cannot) have lunch because we do not have any food.*
9. *I want to go to the library now to read books.*
10. *Do you have breakfast every morning?*

LESSON 145

1. *I have one son (a son), but you have two sons.*
2. *My mother reads two newspapers every morning.*
3. *At work, I have two desks.* OR *At work, I have two offices.*
4. *Do y'all have a newspaper?* (OR, using formal speech) *Do you have a newspaper?*
5. *Yes—I have three newspapers.*
6. *The newspapers are on the table.*
7. *I need to drink water because I am thirsty.*
8. *We have two desks.* OR *We have two offices.*
9. *My brother is not able to (my brother cannot) work today.*
10. *At the restaurant, they have breakfast every morning, and they have dinner every evening/night.*

LESSON 146

1. *My family is in the car.*
2. *The books are in our office.* OR *The books are in our desk.*
3. *We are at the library.*
4. *I want to be at the beach, but I am at work.*
5. *Your cats want to eat now.*
6. *We need to buy food this evening/tonight.*
7. *They need to have dinner because their children are hungry.*
8. *They are going to the store tomorrow to buy food.*
9. *We are not able to (we cannot) go to church today because we do not have a car.*
10. *Your dinner is on the table.*

LESSON 147

1. *The dog is in the house.*
2. *The cats are in the living room.*
3. *My brother is going home tomorrow.*
4. *We are not able to (we cannot) have dinner without a table.*
5. *My mother is not at home today.*
6. *We always eat food at the park.*
7. *Y'all's dogs are in the living room on the table!* (OR, using formal speech) *Your dogs are in the living room on the table!*
8. *My brother is not able to (my brother cannot) go to school today, but he is able to (he can) go to school tomorrow.*
9. *I do not want to read a book today.*
10. *She wants to have dinner at the restaurant this evening/tonight.*

LESSON 148

1. *The food is in the kitchen.*
2. *The table is in the dining room.*
3. *The newspapers are in the living room, on the desk.*
4. *The girls want to go to the mall to see their friends and also to buy clothes.*
5. *We are not able to (we cannot) have dinner without a table.*
6. *You are always at the library, but you never read the books.*
7. *My dad wants his newspaper, but the newspaper is not on his desk.*
8. *We do not have a table in our kitchen, but we have a table in the dining room.*
9. *We need to go to the store to buy a table, but we never have any money.*
10. *My father does not want to go to work today—he wants to go home.*

LESSON 149

1. *My sister is in her bedroom.*
2. *The cats are on my bed.*
3. *Are the children in bed?*
4. *The dogs are on the bed with my parents.*
5. *My bed and my desk are in my bedroom.*
6. *My brothers and my sisters are in the house.*
7. *My brother's bedroom has two beds.*
8. *My father and my mother are in the kitchen, but my sister is in the dining room.*
9. *Your breakfast is on the table in the dining room.*
10. *I never go to school without my books.*

LESSON 150

1. *I sleep in my bed every night.*
2. *We do not want to eat now—we want to sleep!*
3. *The cats sleep in the living room every night.*
4. *I do not want to go to the beach now—I want to sleep in my bed.*
5. *The cats sleep on the bed with the children every night.*
6. *My dog always sleeps on the bed with me.*
7. *He is sleeping in his bedroom.*
8. *The books are on the desk.*
9. *Y'all's friends are in the house, in the living room.* (OR, using formal speech) *Your friends are in the house, in the living room.*
10. *We never have breakfast.*

LESSON 151

1. *She makes lunch every day.*
2. *We are making breakfast now.*
3. *I have breakfast every morning, but you never have breakfast.*
4. *Do they make breakfast every morning?*
5. *I do my job every day, but you always sleep.*
6. *They always make dinner.*
7. *We make dinner in the kitchen, but we have dinner in the dining room.* OR *We are making dinner in the kitchen, but we are having dinner in the dining room.*
8. *My dog always sleeps in the kitchen, but his bed is in the living room.*
9. *The book is in the desk.* OR *The book is in the office.*
10. *You need to go to the mall to buy clothes.*

LESSON 152

1. *I make dinner for my friends every week.*
2. *I want to make lunch for my friends.*
3. *My father does not want to buy a car for my brother.*
4. *My brother is making dinner for his children.*
5. *The children are in bed now.*
6. *Is your mother making dinner this evening/tonight?*
7. *We are not able to (we cannot) have breakfast because the children are sleeping.*
8. *I always sleep in my bedroom.*
9. *My family has dinner in the dining room.* OR *My family is having dinner in the dining room.*
10. *We are a buying a dog for the children, but my husband wants a cat.*

271

LESSON 153

1. *My daughter likes the dog.*
2. *My daughter likes dogs.*
3. *My father does not like cats.*
4. *Do you like to read?*
5. *Yes, I read two books every week.*
6. *I do not like my job.*
7. *We like the house because the house has a dining room and also a living room.*
8. *I am not able to (I cannot) sleep because I do not like my bed.*
9. *I like to make breakfast for my family every morning.*
10. *We have a table in our kitchen.*

LESSON 155

1. *He likes dogs.*
2. *I love my husband.*
3. *We like to read.*
4. *I like to eat at the restaurant every evening/night.*
5. *I love Michael.*
6. *He does not like to work.*
7. *He does not want to work now—he wants to sleep.*
8. *He is making breakfast in the kitchen.*
9. *The food is on the table in the living room.*
10. *They like the house because it has four bedrooms.*

LESSON 156

1. *I like eggs.*
2. *My mother likes bread.*
3. *Y'all like to eat eggs.* (OR, using formal speech) *You like to eat eggs.*
4. *Are the eggs in the kitchen?*
5. *We need to buy eggs and bread tomorrow.*
6. *We are not able to (we cannot) go to the mall because we are having lunch now.*
7. *I love my wife, and she loves me also.*
8. *We eat eggs for breakfast every morning.*
9. *I do not like to sleep in the living room—I like to sleep in my room, in my bed.*
10. *She does not like the house because it does not have three bedrooms.*

LESSON 157

1. *Do you want toast and butter?*
2. *I like toast without butter.*
3. *My sister likes to eat toast and butter for breakfast every morning.*
4. *Do y'all want bread and butter?* (OR, using formal speech) *Do you want bread and butter?*
5. *They like to eat eggs and toast every morning.*
6. *Y'all are not able to (y'all cannot) buy clothes at the mall without money.* (OR, using formal speech) *You are not able to (you cannot) buy clothes at the mall without money.*
7. *My mother is making breakfast this morning.*
8. *The dog sleeps on my bed.* OR *The dog is sleeping on my bed.*
9. *My parents are in the kitchen.*
10. *The children are not at home now.*

LESSON 158

1. *My father does not like to cook.*
2. *My husband always does the cooking.*
3. *My brother wants to cook every evening/night.*
4. *I do the cooking every evening/night, but this evening/tonight I want to go to the restaurant to have dinner.*
5. *They are hungry because they never have breakfast.*
6. *Your food is not on the table—your food is on the desk.*
7. *We are in the living room, but my parents are in the kitchen.*
8. *She cooks every evening/night.*
9. *He is not able to (he cannot) cook today because he is going to work.*
10. *My bed is in my bedroom.*

LESSON 159

1. *My brother eats cereal every morning.*
2. *We want cereal with milk.*
3. *I want to eat cereal with milk.*
4. *Are you eating breakfast now?*
5. *I am not able to (I cannot) carry the books to school every morning.*
6. *Do you want to drink water, Mr. Smith?*
7. *My sister does not like eggs, but she likes cereal with milk.*
8. *My father is eating toast and butter.*
9. *I do not like toast.*
10. *We are going to the mall to eat dinner.*

LESSON 160

1. *We want more milk.*
2. *I need to go to the store because we need more food.*
3. *My family does not like eggs.*
4. *I love Jennifer.*
5. *The children do not like eggs.*
6. *Y'all need to read more books* (OR, using formal speech) *You need to read more books.*
7. *My brother needs to drink more water.*
8. *The cat is in the kitchen.*
9. *I want to eat some bread with my lunch.*
10. *My mother is making dinner for my father.*

LESSON 161

1. *I want some eggs, please.*
2. *We want to eat now, please.*
3. *Are you able to (can you) make breakfast for me, please?*
4. *More toast and cereal, please.*
5. *They like to go to the beach every week.*
6. *Do y'all like to eat eggs?* (OR, using formal speech) *Do you like to eat eggs?*
7. *They often like to read my father's books.*
8. *I need to make breakfast for my children.*
9. *Do you like to go to the park often?*
10. *The dog wants my dinner.*

LESSON 162

1. *I love the beach.*
2. *I like the beach.*
3. *My sister adores Mr. Smith.*
4. *My son loves to do the cooking.*
5. *My brother loves to go to the library and read books.*
6. *Can you work today?*
7. *For breakfast, I love to eat toast and butter.*
8. *My father is not able to (my father cannot) work today.*
9. *She likes to buy clothes at the mall.*
10. *We are going to the restaurant to have dinner.*

LESSON 163

1. *I want to eat a salad for lunch.*
2. *My friends want to eat salad for lunch, but I want to eat a sandwich.*
3. *I like sandwiches.*
4. *I love sandwiches.*
5. *My mother is making salad for lunch.*
6. *My father is eating salad with his dinner.*
7. *My sister wants a car.*
8. *We are going to the library to read books.*
9. *She wants to go to the beach.*
10. *I love you.*

LESSON 164

1. *A (cup of) coffee, please.*
2. *She wants coffee, but I want juice.*
3. *More juice, please.*
4. *My father is making coffee for my mother.*
5. *I love coffee.*
6. *I am not able to (I cannot) sleep because I am drinking coffee.*
7. *I like to drink coffee with my breakfast.*
8. *We drink coffee every morning.*
9. *My sister makes breakfast every morning.*
10. *Do you like your coffee with milk?*

LESSON 166

1. *We need to eat more fruit every day.*
2. *I like to drink orange juice for breakfast.*
3. *My son does not like apple juice.*
4. *The children are eating turkey sandwiches.*
5. *My children love orange juice.*
6. *We do not need to sleep—we need to drink coffee because we need to work.*
7. *I like to eat toast every morning.*
8. *My son likes chicken sandwiches.*
9. *I am not able to (I cannot) drink coffee, but I love juice.*
10. *My friends are going to the park.*

LESSON 167

1. *My mother loves cheese.*
2. *I am eating a cheese sandwich.*
3. *We are going to the restaurant to eat chicken soup.*
4. *He eats soup for dinner every evening/night.*
5. *I want to drink apple juice and orange juice with my breakfast.*
6. *My family loves toast and butter.*
7. *More coffee, please.*
8. *She is not able to (she cannot) go to the park because she is having lunch with her family now.*
9. *My children have breakfast every morning with me.*
10. *Mr. Smith wants to eat a turkey sandwich for lunch every day, but Mrs. Smith likes to eat fruit and a chicken salad.*

LESSON 168

1. *Thank you for the newspaper.*
2. *You're welcome.*
3. *Thank you for the cheese, Mom.*
4. *You're welcome, my son.*
5. *Thank you for the turkey sandwich, Dad.*
6. *You're welcome, my daughter.*
7. *We need more food, please.*
8. *My sisters do not like chicken soup.*
9. *Do you like apple juice?*
10. *This morning, I want orange juice and also fruit for breakfast.*

LESSON 169

1. *My mother is making chicken, vegetables, and potatoes for dinner.*
2. *My dad loves potatoes.*
3. *Mom, I do not want to eat any vegetables.*
4. *My children do not like vegetables.*
5. *I like turkey sandwiches.*
6. *The restaurant has soups, salads, and sandwiches.*
7. *Today, we are eating fruit for breakfast.*
8. *My dad wants to eat a chicken sandwich for lunch, but I want chicken soup.*
9. *Do you like orange juice?*
10. *No, I do not like orange juice, but I love to drink coffee.*

LESSON 170

1. *Is this/that your father?*
2. *Yes, this/that is my father.*
3. *Is this/that your sister?*
4. *No, this/that is not my sister.*
5. *Is this/that cheese?*
6. *No, this/that is orange juice.*
7. *This/that is a cheese sandwich.*
8. *I like potato salad.*
9. *This/that is not a chicken sandwich.*
10. *Thank you for the vegetable soup, Mom.*

LESSON 171

1. *Who is this/that/it? Your dad?*
2. *No, this/that/it is my friend.*
3. *Who is this/that/it? Your friend?*
4. *No, this/that/it is not my friend. This/that/it is my sister.*
5. *My brother wants to read books at the library every week.*
6. *Who is this/that/it? Mr. Smith?*
7. *Yes, Mr. Smith has dinner at the restaurant every evening/night.*
8. *My wife loves to eat chicken salad for lunch every day.*
9. *I like cheese sandwiches.*
10. *I love your sister.*

LESSON 172

1. *What is this/that/it? A chicken sandwich?*
2. *No, this/that/it is a turkey sandwich.*
3. *What is this/that/it? Y'all's house?* (OR, using formal speech) *What is this/that/it? Your house?*
4. *No, this/that/it is not my house. This/that/it is a restaurant!*
5. *Who is this/that/it? Your son?*
6. *My children love apple juice, but I like orange juice.*
7. *A potato is not a fruit—it is a vegetable.*
8. *More cereal, please.*
9. *The cat is eating our chicken salad!*
10. *My dad loves to drink coffee, but I do not like coffee.*

PRONUNCIATION GUIDE

VOWELS

a, à, â sound like the *a* in *father*

e, è, ê, ë sound like the *e* in *bed*

é sounds like the *ay* in *day*

i, î, ï sound like the *ee* in *meet*

o, ô sound like the *o* in *obey*

u, û usually sound like the *u* in *rule*

CONSONANTS

b sounds like the *b* in *boy*

c sounds like the *k* in *kite* in the following combinations: **ca**, **co**, and **cu**

c sounds like the *s* in *seat* in the following combinations: **ce** and **ci**

ç makes a hissing *s* sound

d sounds like the *d* in *door*

f sounds like the *f* in *fox*

g sounds like the *g* in *goat* in the following combinations: **ga**, **go**, and **gu**

g sounds like the *s* in *vision* in the following combinations: **ge** and **gi**

h is always silent unless paired with the letter *c*.

j sounds like the *s* in *vision*

k sounds like the *k* in *kite*

l sounds like the *l* in *lake*

m sounds like the *m* in *mother*

n sounds like the *n* in *nose*

p sounds like the *p* in *pipe*

qu sounds like the *k* in *kite*

r should be slightly and quickly gurgled

s makes a hissing *s* sound, except when it is between two vowels. Then, it makes a *z* sound.

t sounds like the *t* in *take*

v sounds like the *v* in *vase*

w sounds like the *w* in *wash*

x sounds like the *z* in *zap* when it begins a word. It often sounds like the *x* in *fox*.

y sounds like the *y* in *yes* when it's being used as a consonant. It sounds like the *ee* in *meet* when it's being used as a vowel.

z sounds like the *z* in *zap*

GLOSSARY

à *to, at*
acheter *to buy*
adorer *to love*
aimer *to like, to love*
ami / amie *friend*
aller *to go*
argent *money*
aujourd'hui *today*
au revoir *goodbye*
aussi *also*
avec *with*
avoir *to have*
banque *bank*
besoin *need*
beurre *butter*
bibliothèque *library*
boire *to drink*
bonjour *good day*
café *coffee*
centre commercial *mall, shopping center*
céréales *cereal*
c'est *this is, that is, it is*
cinq *five*
chambre (à coucher) *bedroom*
chat *cat*
chien *dog*
cuisine *kitchen, cooking*
dans *in*
déjeuner *lunch*
demain *tomorrow*
des *some*
deux *two*
dinde *turkey*
dîner *dinner*
dix *ten*
dormir *to sleep*
douze *twelve*
eau *water*
école *school*

église *church*
elle *she, her*
elles *they, them* (female)
enfant *child*
es *are*
est *is*
est-ce que? *is it that?*
et *and*
êtes *are*
eux *them*
faim *hunger*
faire *to do, to make*
famille *family*
femme *woman, wife*
fille *girl, daughter*
fils *son*
frère *brother*
fromage *cheese*
fruit *fruit*
garçon *boy*
homme *man*
huit *eight*
il *he*
ils *they*
jamais *never*
je *I*
jour *day*
journal *newspaper*
jus *juice*
la *the, her, it*
lait *milk*
le *the, him, it*
légume *vegetable*
les *the, them*
leur/leurs *their*
lire *to read*
lit *bed*
livre *book*
lui *him*
madame *Mrs., ma'am*

mademoiselle *miss*
magasin *store*
maintenant *now*
mais *but*
maison *house*
manger *to eat*
matin *morning*
me *me*
merci *thank you*
mère *mother*
moi *me*
mon/ma *my*
monsieur *Mr., sir*
ne…pas *not*
neuf *nine*
non *no*
nos *our*
notre *our*
nourriture *food*
nous *we, us*
œuf *egg*
onze *eleven*
orange *orange*
oui *yes*
pain *bread*
pain grillé *toast*
parc *park*
parce que *because*
parent *parent*
parler *to speak*
père *father*
petit déjeuner *breakfast*
plage *beach*
plus de *more*
pomme *apple*
pomme de terre *potato*
porter *to carry*
poulet *chicken*
pour *for*
pouvoir *to be able*
quatre *four*
qu'est-ce que c'est? *what is it?*
qui est-ce? *who is this?*

restaurant *restaurant*
riz *rice*
salade *salad*
salle à manger *dining room*
salon *living room*
sandwich *sandwich*
sans *without*
sept *seven*
s'il vous plaît *please*
six *six*
sœur *sister*
soif *thirst*
soir *evening, night*
son/sa *his, her*
sont *are*
sommes *are*
soupe *soup*
souvent *often*
suis *am*
sur *on*
te *you*
toi *you*
ton/ta *your*
toujours *always*
tous les jours *every day*
tous les matins *every morning*
toutes les semaines *every week*
tous les soirs *every night, every evening*
travail *work, job*
travailler *to work*
trois *three*
tu *you* (singular)
un *a, an, one*
une *a, an*
vêtements *clothes*
voiture *car*
vos *y'all's* or, in formal speech, *your*
votre *y'all's* or, in formal speech, *your*
vouloir *to want*
vous *y'all* or, in formal speech, *you*
voir *to see*
zéro *zero*

SUBJECT INDEX

A

articles, lesson 3, 5, 8, 11, 13, 31, 37, 38, 61, 65, 66, 76

D

direct objects, lesson 112, 113, 114

E

elision, lesson 19, 20
enchaînment, lesson 21

F

formal speech, lesson 50

G

gender, lesson 4, 30

I

idioms, lesson 82
infinitives, lesson 121, 123, 124

L

liaison, lesson 22, 23

N

negation, lesson 44, 76

P

partitive article lesson 66, 76
person lesson 54
personal endings, lesson 90, 91
plural, lesson 28, 30, 31, 146
possession, lesson 79, 80, 81
prepositions, lesson 101, 102, 104, 106
present tense, lesson 88
pronouns, lesson 42, 43, 107, 113, 114, 118
pronunciation, lesson 1, 2, 6, 14, 16, 17, 19, 20, 21, 22, 23
purpose, lesson 136, 137

Q

questions, lesson 93, 94

S

singular, lesson 28
stressed pronouns, lesson 107
subjects, lesson 41

T

titles, lesson 48

V

verb stems, lesson 90, 124
verbs, lesson 41

CPSIA information can be obtained
at www.ICGtesting.com
Printed in the USA
BVHW02s0201131217
502611BV00001B/12/P